我的人生美文
那些随风飘远的日子

英汉对照　词汇解析　语法讲解　励志语录

马琼琼　编著

中国纺织出版社

图书在版编目（CIP）数据

我的人生美文：那些随风飘逝的日子：英文／马琼琼编著． -- 北京：中国纺织出版社，2019.4
　　ISBN 978-7-5180-5093-2

Ⅰ．①我… Ⅱ．①马… Ⅲ．①英语—语言读物②散文集—世界 Ⅳ．① H319.4：Ⅰ

中国版本图书馆 CIP 数据核字（2018）第 116712 号

责任编辑：武洋洋　　责任校对：武凤余　　责任印制：储志伟

中国纺织出版社出版发行
地址：北京市朝阳区百子湾东里A407号楼　邮政编码：100124
销售电话：010—67004422　传真：010—87155801
http://www.c-textilep.com
E-mail:faxing@c-textilep.com
中国纺织出版社天猫旗舰店
官方微博http://www.weibo.com/2119887771
三河市延风印装有限公司印刷　各地新华书店经销
2019年4月第1版第1次印刷
开本：880×1230　1/32　印张：6.5
字数：210千字　定价：39.80元

凡购本书，如有缺页、倒页、脱页，由本社图书营销中心调换

前言

思想结晶改变人生命运，经典美文提高生活品位。曾几何时，一个字，触动你的心弦；一句话，让你泪流满面；一篇短文，让你重拾信心，勇敢面对生活给你的考验。这就是语言的魅力。通过阅读优美的英文短文，不仅能够扩大词汇量，掌握单词的用法，了解语法，学习地道的表达，更让你的心灵如沐春风，得到爱的呵护和情感的滋养。

岁月流转，经典永存。针对英语学习爱好者的需要，编者精心选取了难易适中的英语经典美文，为你提供一场丰富多彩的文学盛宴。本书采用中英文对照的形式，便于读者理解。每篇美文后都附有单词解析、语法知识点、经典名句三大版块，让你在欣赏完一篇美文后，还能扩充词汇量、巩固语法知识、斟酌文中好句，并感悟人生。在一篇篇不同题材风格的英语美文中，你总能找到引起你心灵共鸣的一篇。

读一本新书恰似坠入爱河，是场冒险。你得全身心地投入进去。翻开书页之时，从前言直至封底你或许都知之甚少。但谁又不是呢？字里行间的只言片语不总是正确的。

有时候你会发现，人们自我推销时是一种形象，等你在深入了解后，他们就完全变样了。有时故事的叙述流于表面，朴实的语言，平淡的情节，但阅读过半后，你却发觉这本书真是出乎意料的妙不可言，而这种感受只能靠自己去感悟！

阅读之乐，腹有诗书气自华；阅读之美，活水云影共天光。阅读可以放逐百年孤独，阅读可以触摸千年月光。阅读中有眼前的收获，阅读中也有诗和远方。

　　让我们静下心来感受英语美文的温度，在英语美文中仔细品味似曾相识的细腻情感，感悟生命和人性的力量。

编者
2018年6月

目录

01 Everybody Can Be Great
　天生我才必有用 ································· 001

02 Big Rocks
　人生的大石头 ································· 007

03 Books
　书籍 ··· 013

04 The World As I See It
　我的世界观 ··································· 019

05 Old Shoes, Happy Life
　旧鞋子也有温暖 ······························· 026

06 A Lesson of Life
　生活的一课 ··································· 032

07 Keep Your Fork
　紧握餐叉 ····································· 037

08 The Enchantment of Creeks
　小溪的魅力 ··································· 043

09 Sleeping Through the Storm
　未雨绸缪 ····································· 049

10 A Little at a Time
　循序渐进 ····································· 054

11 If the Dream Is Big Enough
　如果梦想足够远大 ····························· 060

12 Two Roads
　两条道路 ····································· 067

13 The Answer Is Right There Above You
希望就在前方 ·················· 073

14 Great Expectations
最高期望值 ·················· 079

15 Mirror, Mirror—What Do I See?
镜子，镜子，告诉我 ·················· 085

16 How to Be True to Yourself
如何做个表里如一的人 ·················· 091

17 If I Were A Boy Again
假如回到童年 ·················· 097

18 If I Rest I Rust
如果我休息，我就会生锈 ·················· 103

19 The Metal of Life
生活的奖牌 ·················· 108

20 Rules of Credibility
诚信的规则 ·················· 114

21 A Good Heart to Lean On
善心可依 ·················· 120

22 The Gold in the Orchard
果园里的金子 ·················· 126

23 Companionship of Books
以书为伴 ·················· 132

24 College—A Transition Point in My Life
大学——我生命中的转折点 ·················· 137

25 Weakness or Strength
弱点还是强项 ·················· 143

26 Feed Your Mind
别让你的脑子挨饿 ·················· 149

27 Run Out of the Rainy Season of Your Life
跑出人生的雨季 ·················· 156

Contents 目录

28 Eating the Cookie
生活的真谛 ·· 162

29 Love Your Life
热爱生活 ·· 168

30 Choosing an Occupation
选择职业 ·· 173

31 The Rose Within
带刺的玫瑰 ·· 179

32 My Pain
我的痛苦 ·· 185

33 Draw a Leaf for Life
为生命画一片叶 ·· 191

01 Everybody Can Be Great
天生我才必有用

Mark was walking home from school one day when he noticed that the boy ahead of him had **tripped** and dropped all of the books he was carrying, along with two sweaters, a baseball bat, a glove and a small tape recorder. Mark **knelt** down and helped the boy pick up the **scattered** articles. Since they were going the same way, he helped to carry part of the burden. As they walked, Mark discovered that the boy's name was Bill, that he loved video games, baseball and history that he was having a lot of trouble with his other subjects and that he had just broken up with his girlfriend.

They arrived at Bill's home first and Mark was invited in for a Coke and to watch some television. The afternoon passed pleasantly with a few laughs and some shared small talk, then Mark went home. They continued to see each other around school, had lunch together once or twice, and then both graduated from junior high school. They ended up in the same high school where they had brief **contacts** over the years. Finally the long **awaited** senior year came, and three

一天马克在从学校回家的路上，看到一个男孩走在他前面，被绊了一下，书都掉了，还有两件毛衣、一个棒球棒、一副手套和一个小录音机。马克跪在地上帮那个男孩捡这些零散的东西。因为他们走一条路，马克就帮他拿点东西，分担一下。他们一边走一边聊，马克知道了那个男孩叫贝尔，他喜欢电子游戏、棒球，还知道了他以前其他事情都不顺，而且刚跟女朋友分手。

他们先到了贝尔的家，马克被邀请进去喝杯可乐、看会儿电视。那个下午他们过得很快乐，伴随着欢笑和闲谈。然后马克就回家了。他们继续在学校附近见面，偶尔吃一两次午饭，然后一起从初中毕业了。他们后来上了同一所高中，在那里他们保持了多年联系。最后，在期待中高三来了，毕业前三周，贝尔问马克能不能聊聊天。

贝尔提起了多年前那天他们初次相遇的情景。贝尔问："你知道为什么那天我拿着那

001

weeks before graduation, Bill asked Mark if they could talk.

  Bill reminded him of the day years ago when they had first met. "Do you ever wonder why I was carrying so many things home that day?" asked Bill. "You see, cleaned out my locker because I didn't want to leave a mess for anyone else. I had stored away some of my mother's sleeping pills and I was going home to **commit** suicide. But after we spent some time together talking and laughing, I realized that if I had killed myself, I would have missed that time and so many others that might follow. So you see, Mark, when you picked up my books that day, you did a lot more. You saved my life."

么多东西回家吗？你知道，我清理柜子是因为不想给别人留下一堆混乱的东西。我自己储存了一些我妈妈的安眠药，我就是要回家自杀。但是在我们一起说话、大笑之后，我意识到，如果我自杀了，我会错过之后的很多时间、很多人和事情。所以，你看，马克，当你那天捡起我的书时，你不只做了这些。你救了我的命。"

单词解析 Word Analysis

trip [trɪp] *vt.* 使跌倒；使失败；使犯错；起锚 *vi.* 绊倒；旅行；轻快地走；失误；结巴

例 He tripped on a tree root.
　　他被一株树根绊倒了。

knelt [nelt] *vi.* 跪（kneel的过去式和过去分词）

例 He knelt in front of the emperor with a look of entreaty.
　　他面带恳求的神态跪在皇帝面前。

kneel [niːl] *v.* 跪

例 Do not kneel, go straight to your feet.
　　千万不要跪着，要站直。

Everybody Can Be Great
天生我才必有用 01

scattered ['skætərd] *adj.* 分散的；稀疏的

例 His land is split up into several widely scattered plots.
他的土地被分割成相当分散的几小块。

contact ['kɑːntækt] *n.* 接触；联系；熟人

例 The rich secluded themselves from contact with the poor.
富人不肯同穷人接触。

await [ə'weɪt] *v.* 等候；期待；将降临于

例 We eagerly await your early arrival.
我们殷切地期待你早日光临。

commit [kə'mɪt] *v.* 犯罪；承诺；委托；托付

例 He committed suicide rather than sell out to the enemy.
他宁愿自杀也没有向敌人投降。

语法知识点 Grammar points

① **Mark was walking home from school one day when he noticed that the boy ahead of him had tripped and dropped all of the books he was carrying, along with two sweaters, a baseball bat, a glove and a small tape recorder.**

这个句子中有一个when引导的时间状语从句，和一个that引导的宾语从句，从句做notice的宾语。

ahead of 在……前面；先于

例 A still better tomorrow lies ahead of you.
展现在你们前面的是更加美好的未来。

trip：我们都知道trip的意思是"旅行"，是名词。而在这里，trip做动词，表示"绊倒"的意思。

例 He tripped on a tree root.
他被一株树根绊倒了。

along with 与……在一起；在……以外；沿着；随着；（除……之外）又……，加之

003

例 An ambulance was racing along with its sirens wailing.
救护车响着警报急驰而过。
The man walked along with an unsteady gait.
那人脚步不稳地向前走去。

② **Mark knelt down and helped the boy pick up the scattered articles.**

kneel down 跪下
例 The subjects had to kneel down before the king.
在国王的面前臣民必须跪下。
pick up 捡起；收集；继续；得到；接人；偶然结识；站起，扶起；学会；逮捕；振作精神
例 He picked up his knife and fork.
他捡起了刀叉。
He picked up the child and put her on his shoulders.
他抱起孩子让她骑在自己的肩膀上。
article：article有很多意思，我们常见的是"文章""论文""报道"等。本文里，article表示"物件"的意思。
例 She asked him to contribute a biweekly article on European affairs.
她让他每两周写一篇有关欧洲情况的文章。
If you don't return the article to the shop within a week, you forfeit your chance of getting your money back.
如果你不把物品归还商店，你就丧失了取回钱的机会。

③ **As they walked, Mark discovered that the boy's name was Bill, that he loved video games, baseball and history that he was having a lot of trouble with his other subjects and that he had just broken up with his girlfriend.**

这个句子中有一个as引导的时间状语从句，和一个that引导的宾语从句，从句做discover的宾语；还有一个that引导的同位语从句，先行词是history，从句是对history的补充说明，that在从句中不充当任何成分。

Everybody Can Be Great
天生我才必有用

break up：break是"打碎"的意思。break up在这里表示"终止""破裂"的意思。指男孩子与女朋友断绝了关系。另外，break up还有一个很有趣的含义，表示"大笑"，是那种忍俊不禁、突然爆发出来的笑声。

例 They decided to break up the partnership.
他们决定终止合作关系。

④ **I had stored away some of my mother's sleeping pills and I was going home to commit suicide.**

store away：或store up，意思是"把……储存起来""储备"。

例 Memory is a child walking along seashore. You can never tell what small pebble it will pick up and store away among its treasured things.
记忆犹如一个沿着海边行走的孩子。你永远无法知道它会拣起哪块小石头珍藏起来。

经典名句 Famous Classics

1. I believe that imagination is stronger than knowledge. That myth is more potent than history. That dreams are more powerful than facts. That hope always triumphs over experience. That laughter is the only cure for grief. And I believe that love is stronger than death.
我相信想象力比知识更为强大，神话比历史影响更加深远，梦想比现实更加有力。希望总是胜过经验。笑声是悲伤的唯一良药。我也相信爱比死亡更强大。

2. We tend to forget that happiness doesn't come as a result of getting something we don't have, but rather of recognizing and appreciating what we do have.
我们总是忘记：幸福不是得到我们没有的，而是认可、欣赏我们此刻拥有的。

3. Happiness grows at our own firesides, and is not to be picked in strangers' gardens.
幸福生长在我们自己的火炉边，而不能从别人的花园中采得。

4. It is better that ten guilty persons escape than one innocent suffer.
   宁肯放过十个有罪之人，也不让一个无辜的人受苦。

5. The most beautiful thing we can experience is the mysterious. It is the source of all true art and science.
   我们能体验的最美好的东西都是神秘的。这是真正的艺术与科学的来源。

6. Often people attempt to live their lives backwards; they try to have more things, or more money, in order to do more of what they want, so they will be happier. The way it actually works is the reverse. You must first be who you really are, then do what you need to do, in order to have what you want.
   人们通常竭尽全力让自己生活的好一点；他们想要得到更多东西或金钱，得到的多了，他们也就幸福了。但事实上相反。一个人，首先要做自己，然后完成分内的事情，再得到自己想要的。

02 Big Rocks
人生的大石头

One day, an expert in time management was speaking to a group of students and, to drive home a point, used an **illustration** those students will never forget.

As he stood in front of the group of **overachievers** he said, "OK, time for a quiz." He pulled out a one-**gallon**, wide-mouth jar and set it on the table in front of him. He also produced about a dozen fist-sized rocks and carefully placed them, one at a time, into the jar. When the jar was filled to the top and no more rocks would fit inside, he asked, "Is this jar full?"

Everyone in the class **yelled**, "Yes." The time management expert replied, "Really?" He reached under the table and pulled out a bucket of **gravel**. He dumped some gravel in and shook the jar, causing pieces of gravel to work themselves down into the spaces between the big rocks. He then asked the group once more, "Is this jar full?"

By this time the class was on to him. "Probably not," one of them answered. "Good!" he replied. He reached under the table and brought out a bucket of sand. He started **dumping**

一天,一个时间管理方面的专家为一群学生讲课。他现场做了演示,给学生们留下了一生都难以磨灭的印象。

站在那些高智商高学历的学生前面,他说"我们来做个小测验",他拿出一个一加仑的广口瓶放在他面前的桌上。随后,他取出一堆拳头大小的石块,仔细地一块一块放进玻璃瓶。直到石块高出瓶口,再也放不下了,他问道:"瓶子满了吗?"

所有学生应道:"满了!"时间管理专家反问:"真的?"他伸手从桌下拿出一桶碎石,倒了一些进去,并敲击玻璃瓶壁使碎石填满下面石块的间隙。"现在瓶子满了吗?"他第二次问道。

但这一次学生有些明白了,"可能还没有。"一位学生应道。"很好!"专家说。他伸手从桌下拿出一桶沙子,开始慢慢倒进玻璃瓶。沙子填满了石块和碎石的所有间隙。他又一次问学生:"瓶子满了吗?"

"没满!"学生们大声说。他再一次说:"很好!"

the sand in the jar and it went into all of the spaces left between the rocks and the gravel. Once more he asked the question, "Is this jar full?"

"No!" the class shouted. Once again he said, "Good." Then he grabbed a **pitcher** of water and began to pour it in until the jar was filled to the **brim**. Then he looked at the class and asked, "What is the point of this illustration?" One eager student raised his hand and said, "The point is, no matter how full your schedule is, if you try really hard, you can always fit some more things in it!"

"No," the speaker replied, "that's not the point". The truth this illustration teaches us is if you don't put the big rocks in first, you'll never get them in at all. What are the 'big rocks' in your life? In my life they are my children... my wife... my loved ones... my education... my dreams... charities and **worthy** causes... teaching or mentoring others... doing things that I love... time for myself... my health. Remember to put these BIG ROCKS in first or you'll never get them in at all."

然后他拿过一壶水倒进玻璃瓶直到水面与瓶口齐平。抬头看着学生，问道："这个例子说明什么？"一个心急的学生举手发言："无论你的时间多少，如果你确实努力，你可以做更多的事情！"

"回答得好，不过，"专家说，"这不是我想说的。这个例子告诉我们一个事实：如果你不是先放大石块，以后它们就永远摆不进去。你生活中的'大石块'是什么呢？在我的生活中，那就是我的孩子、妻子、所爱的人、学习、梦想、善行和有价值的事业、教导他人、做我喜欢做的事、留给自己的时间、健康等。要记住，必须先放'大石块'，否则它们永远放不进去。"

单词解析 Word Analysis

illustration [ˌɪləˈstreɪʃn] *n.* 说明；例证；图解；插图

例 Perhaps the accompanying illustration will explain it.
可能所附的图表能对此做出解释。

Big Rocks 人生的大石头 02

overachiever [ˌəʊvərəˈtʃiːvə(r)] *n.* 成绩超过预料的学生；成就比预期更大的人

例 In fact, small colonies may sometimes rely on a single hyperactive overachiever.
有时，一个小蚁群可能依靠一只能力超强的个体生存。

gallon [ˈɡælən] *n.* 加仑（容量单位）

例 The imperial gallon is not the same size as the US one.
英制的加仑与美制的容量不同。

yell [jel] *v.* 喊叫着说

例 "Please don't yell at me." She began to sniffle.
"请不要对我大喊大叫。"她啜泣起来。

gravel [ˈɡrævl] *n.* 沙砾；碎石

例 Two young men were racing motorcycles on the loose gravel.
两个小伙子正在松散的砾石路面上赛摩托车。

dump [dʌmp] *v.* 倾倒；倾卸

例 The government declared that it did not dump radioactive waste at sea.
政府宣称并未将放射性废料倾倒在海里。

pitcher [ˈpɪtʃə(r)] *n.* 投手；大水罐

例 Any pitcher is liable to crack during a tight game.
任何投手在紧张的比赛中都可能会失常。

brim [brɪm] *n.* 边；边缘

例 Richard filled her glass right up to the brim.
理查德给她倒了满满一杯。

worthy [ˈwɜːði] *adj.* 值得的，配得上的；有价值的

例 There occurred nothing that was worthy to be mentioned.
没有值得一提的事发生。

我的人生美文：那些随风飘逝的日子

语法知识点 *Grammar points*

① **One day, an expert in time management was speaking to a group of students and, to drive home a point, used an illustration those students will never forget.**

drive home 使人理解

例 Speaking to a small group of reporters here in Riyadh, the president sought to drive home the impact higher oil prices are having in the United States and elsewhere.
在对利雅德的一小群记者讲话时，总统谈了高油价对美国和其他国家的影响。

② **By this time the class was on to him. "Probably not, " one of them answered. "Good! " he replied. He reached under the table and brought out a bucket of sand.**

be on to sb. 找某人的茬

例 The reason for the quarrel was they were on to each other.
他们争吵的原因是它们互相找对方的茬。

③ **One eager student raised his hand and said, "The point is, no matter how full your schedule is, if you try really hard, you can always fit some more things in it! "**

no matter how 无论如何；不管怎样

例 No matter how strenuous the work was, no complaint ever passed her lips.
不论工作多艰巨，她从来没有怨言。

no matter 后除了可以加 how，还可以跟其他的特殊疑问词，如 what、when 等等。

例 No matter what you say, I won't believe you.
不管你说什么，我都相信你。

例 You shouldn't give up your child no matter what he wants.
无论他想怎么样，你都不应该放弃孩子。

Big Rocks 02
人生的大石头

经典名句 Famous Classics

1. When I am dead, my dearest, Sing no sad songs for me; Plant thou no roses at my head, Nor shady cypress tree: Be the green grass above me, With showers and dewdrops wet; And if thou wilt, remember, And if thou wilt, forget.
当我死去时，我亲爱的，不要为我唱哀伤的挽歌；不要在我墓前种上玫瑰，或是阴郁的柏树：请你成为我墓前的绿草吧，带着骤雨的雨水和湿润的露珠；如果你愿意，请记得，如果你愿意，请忘怀。

2. Youth is the time to go flashing from one end of the world to the other both in mind and body; to try the manners of different nations; to hear the chimes at midnight; to see sunrise in town and country; to be converted at a revival; to circumnavigate the metaphysics, write halting verses, run a mile to see a fire, and wait all day long in the theatre to applaud *Hernani*.
年轻的时候，就应该跑遍世界去展示自己的心灵与身体；去体验不同国度的生活；在午夜时聆听钟声敲响；在城镇乡村欣赏日出的景色；在训道时受到感化；看遍形而上学的著作，创作一些不完美的诗歌，跑很远的路去看一场焰火，在剧院里等上一天，只为了为《欧那尼》鼓掌欢呼。

3. Do not look back. And do not dream about the future, either. It will neither give you back the past, nor satisfy your other daydreams. Your duty, your reward—your destiny—are here and now.
不要总是回顾过去，也不要总是梦想未来。这样做既不会让你回到过去，也不会实现你的美梦。你的责任，你的回报——你的命运——就在当下。

4. One is never as unhappy as one thinks, or as happy as one hopes to be.
一个人永远不会像自己想象的一样不幸，也永远不会像自己希望的一样幸福。

5. When I think of all the books I have read, and of the wise words I have heard spoken, and of the anxiety I have given to parents and

grandparents, and of the hopes that I have had, all life weighed in the scales of my own life seems to me preparation for something that never happens.

当我回顾我曾经读过的书，曾经听过的箴言警句，曾经给长辈带来的烦恼，曾经有过的希冀，我的整个生命衡量起来，仿佛是在为什么从未发生的事情做准备。

6. We combat obstacles in order to get repose, and, when got, the repose is insupportable.

我们为了得到安宁而去战胜阻碍，当我们终于成功时，却不堪忍受这种安宁。

7. Friendship is tested in the thick years of success rather than in the thin years of struggle.

比起清贫单薄的日子，友谊在功成名就的富足生活中要经受更大的考验。

8. We cherish our friends not for their ability to amuse us, but for our ability to amuse them.

我们爱我们的朋友并非因为他们能逗笑我们，而是因为我们能够逗笑他们。

9. True happiness is of a retired nature, and an enemy to pomp and noise; it arises, in the first place, from the enjoyment of one's self, and in the next from the friendship and conversation of a few select companions.

真正的幸福是不张扬的，它摒弃炫耀与喧嚣；幸福首先来源于对自我的欣赏，其次来源于与挚友之间的友谊以及交谈。

10. I have had, and may have still, a thousand friends, as they are called, in life, who are like one's partners in the waltz of this world—not much remembered when the ball is over.

我的人生中有过，并且仍然会有上千个所谓的朋友。而他们就像是我们在世上的舞伴，舞会结束后就被遗忘了。

03 Books
书籍

The good books of the hour, then, —I do not speak of the bad ones—are simply the useful or pleasant talk of some person whom you cannot otherwise **converse** with, printed for you. Very useful often, telling you what you need to know; very pleasant often, as a sensible friend's present talk would be. These bright accounts of travels; good-humored and **witty** discussion of questions; lively or **pathetic** story-telling in the form of novel; firm fact-telling, by the real agents concerned in the events of passing history—all these books of the hour, multiplying among us as education becomes more general, are a **peculiar** characteristic and possession of the present age: we ought to be entirely thankful for them, and entirely ashamed of ourselves if we make no good use of them. But we make the worse possible use, if we allow them to **usurp** the place of true books: for, strictly speaking, they are not books at all, but merely letters or newspapers in good print. Our friend's letter may be delightful, or necessary, today, whether worth keeping or not is to be considered.

读一个小时的好书——我指的是好书，就像跟一个你无法交谈的人进行了一场有用的、开心的对话一样，只不过是印刷了出来。通常来说，很有用是因为书告诉你你需要了解的事情；很开心是因为就像跟一个明智的朋友现实对话一样。这些明亮鲜活的游记，充满幽默感和智慧的对问题的探讨，以小说的形式生动、感伤地讲述故事，对以往历史事件关注的新闻当事人的严格写实——随着教育越来越普遍，我们读的这些书也加倍增长，成为当今社会一种特色和财富。我们应该感谢这些书籍，如果我们没能好好利用它们，我们应该感到羞愧。但是如果我们让它们篡夺了真正的书籍的地位，那我们可能更坏地利用了它们。因为，严格说来，它们不是书，只是印刷得很好的信件或报纸。一个朋友的来信可能是让人高兴的，或是必要的，现在是否值得保留信件，值得思考。

报纸在早餐时间读应该是

The newspaper may be entirely proper at breakfast time, but **assuredly** it is not reading for all day. So though bound up in a volume, the long letter which gives you so pleasant an account of the **inns**, the roads, and weather last year at such a place, or which tells you that amusing story, or gives you the real circumstances of such and such events, however valuable for occasional reference, may not be, in the real sense of the word, a "book" at all, nor, in the real sense, to be "read". A book is essentially not a talked thing, but a written thing; and written, not with the view of mere communication, but of **permanence**.

The author has something to say which he perceives to be true and useful, or helpfully beautiful. So far as he knows, no one has yet said it; so far as he knows, no one else can say it. He is bound to say it, clearly and **melodiously** if he may; clearly, at all events. In the sum of his life he finds this to be the thing, or group of things, **manifest** to him; this piece of true knowledge, or sight, which his share of sunshine and earth has permitted him to seize. He would **fain** set it down for ever; **engrave** it on rock, if he could, saying, "this is the best of me; for the rest, I ate, and drank, and slept, loved and hated, like another; my life was as the **vapor**, and is not; but

最适合的，但是肯定不适合全天阅读。所以，尽管被绑在了一起，那些长信记叙了你去年在这么一个地方，那的客栈、道路以及天气，让你看到都觉得开心的回忆；或者是向你讲述了一个好玩的故事，或者给你某件事情的情景再现，然而不管有多少参考价值，可能这本"书"都不在真实感受的世界中，你也并没有读。本质上来说，书不是谈话，而是写下来的东西；而且写下来的，不只是谈话的观点，还有永久的记忆。

作者有一些他觉得真实的、有用的或美丽的事情要说。据他所知，没有人说过这些；而且没有人可以说出这些话。他一定要说出来，尽他所能清晰地、曼妙地说出来，比任何事情都清晰。在他整个生命历程中，他发现这是一件或是一些他非常明白的事，他对阳光对地球的分享允许他去抓住这些真实的知识碎片或光芒。他会高兴地永远放下它，如果他可以；他会刻在岩石上，写道："这是最好的我；其余的部分，我像其他人一样吃、喝、睡觉，有爱有恨；我的生活像水蒸气但又不是，但这就是我看到的、知道的东西：如果我的任何东西，值得你

this I saw and knew: this, if anything of mine, is worth your memory." That is his "writing"; it is, in his small human way, and with whatever degree of true inspiration in him, his **inscription**, or **scripture**. That is a "Book".

的记忆。"这就是他的作品，确实是，用他渺小的人类的方式，加上他内心无论什么程度的真实的灵感，他的题字，或者文稿。这就是"书籍"。

单词解析 Word Analysis

converse [kən'vɜːrs] *n.* 交谈；谈话
例 It is a pleasure to converse with her.
和她谈话是一种乐趣。

witty ['wɪti] *adj.* 机智的；诙谐的
例 She responded to their criticism with a witty retort.
她以机智的反驳回应了他们的批评。

pathetic [pə'θetɪk] *adj.* 可怜的；不足的；感伤的；悲哀的
例 We saw the pathetic sight of starving children.
我们看到挨饿的儿童悲惨可怜的样子。

peculiar [pɪ'kjuːliər] *adj.* 奇怪的；特殊的；独特的；古怪的
例 The food has a peculiar taste.
这食物有种怪味道。

usurp [juː'zɜːrp] *v.* 篡夺；霸占；篡位
例 You must not allow it to usurp a disproportionate share of your interest.
你不应让它过多地占据你的兴趣。

assuredly [ə'ʃʊərədli] *adv.* 确实地；确信地
例 Assuredly he didn't mean that.
确实他并没有那个意思。

我的人生美文：那些随风飘逝的日子

inn [ɪn] *n.* 客栈；小旅店
例 The traveler decided to lie at an inn that night.
旅行者决定那天晚上在一个小旅店过夜。

permanence ['pɜːrmənəns] *n.* 永久；持久
例 We believe the permanence of the sun.
我们相信太阳的永恒。

melodiously [mə'ləʊdiəsli] *adv.* 旋律美妙地
例 The crashing sound still kept drifting melodiously to distant places.
钟声依然悠悠地传向远方。

manifest ['mænɪfest] *adj.* 明白的；显然的
例 It is now manifest that, if you don't return the book to the library right now, you will have to pay a late fine.
现在情况已很清楚，如果你不立刻把书送回图书馆，你将必须付过时不还书的罚金。

fain [feɪn] *adv.* 乐意地；欣然地
例 I would fain help you.
我乐意帮助你。

engrave [ɪn'greɪv] *v.* 雕刻；刻上；铭记
例 His memorial was engraved on the stone.
纪念他的碑文刻在石碑上。

vapor ['veɪpə] *n.* 蒸汽；水蒸气
例 The locomotive vomits out vapor when getting started.
火车头启动时喷出大量蒸汽。

inscription [ɪn'skrɪpʃn] *n.* 题字；碑铭；铭文
例 He carved an inscription on a bench.
他将一则题字刻在长凳上。

scripture ['skrɪptʃər] *v.* 经文
例 You've read about them in scripture.
你曾经在经文中读到关于他们的事。

语法知识点 *Grammar points*

① **The good books of the hour, then, —I do not speak of the bad ones—is simply the useful or pleasant talk of some person whom you cannot otherwise converse with, printed for you.**

这个句子中，I do not speak of the bad ones做插入语。后面还有一个whom引导的定语从句，修饰先行词some person，whom在从句中充当宾语成分。

speak of 谈到；论及

例 She has saved a little money, but nothing to speak of.
她存了一点钱，但少得不值一提。

converse with 跟某人谈话

例 It is a pleasure to converse with her.
和她谈话是一种乐趣。

② **We ought to be entirely thankful for them, and entirely ashamed of ourselves if we make no good use of them.**

这个句子中有一个if引导的条件状语。

ought to 应当

例 Regularity ought to be observed, as regularity is very conductive to health.
生活应遵守规律，因为规律对健康有益。

be thankful for 对……感激

例 Let us be thankful for the fools; but for them the rest of us could not succeed.
让我们感谢那些蠢材吧，要不是他们，我们就没得成功啦。

ashamed of 惭愧，难为情，羞愧

例 He was so ashamed of his fault that he committed suicide.
他对自己的过错深以为耻，所以自杀身亡。

make good use of 很好利用

例 Those who can't make good use of time are unlikely to go far.
不会好好利用时间的人是不可能大有作为的。

我的人生美文：那些随风飘逝的日子

经典名句 *Famous Classics*

1. The life of every man is a diary in which he means to write one story, and writes another; and his humblest hour is when he compares the volume as it is with what he vowed to make it.
   每个人的生活都是他自己写的一个故事，而他曾誓愿要写的却往往是另外一个故事。人们将这两个故事相互比较的时候，往往让他们自惭形秽。

2. Life is like playing a violin solo in public and learning the instrument as one goes on.
   生活就像是一边学习演奏，一边当众演奏小提琴。

3. What is called the serenity of age is only perhaps a euphemism for the fading power to feel the sudden shock of joy or sorrow
   上了年纪的人所谓的冷静沉着，也许只是一种委婉说法：实际上是因为他们对欢乐与悲伤的感知能力衰退了。

4. As you pass from the tender years of youth into harsh and embittered manhood, make sure you take with you on your journey all the human emotions! Don't leave them on the road, for you will not pick them up afterwards!
   在你从敏感的青春走向残酷现实的成年时，记得在这途中带好你全部的情感！不要把它们丢在路上，因为以后你就无法将它们捡回来了！

5. We face the question whether a still higher "standard of living" is worth its cost in things natural, wild, and free.
   我们面对的问题之一是：所谓"更高水平的生活"是否值得我们放弃自然的、充满野性和自由的生活。

6. Seize the day! Put no trust in the morrow.
   抓住眼前的光阴！不要相信明天。

04 The World As I See It
我的世界观

How strange is the lot of us **mortals**! Each of us is here for a brief **sojourn**; for what purpose he knows not, though he sometimes thinks he senses it. But without deeper reflection one knows from daily life that one exists for other people—first of all for those upon whose smiles and well-being our own happiness is wholly dependent, and then for the many, unknown to us, to whose destinies we are bound by the ties of sympathy. A hundred times every day I remind myself that my inner and outer life are based on the labors of other men, living and dead, and that I must exert myself in order to give in the same measure as I have received and am still receiving. I am strongly drawn to a frugal life and am often **oppressively** aware that I am engrossing an undue amount of the labor of my fellow-men. I regard class **distinctions** as **unjustified** and, in the last resort, based on force. I also believe that a simple and unassuming life is good for everybody, physically and mentally.

I do not at all believe in human freedom in the **philosophical** sense.

我们这些总有一死的人的命运多么奇特！我们每个人在这个世界上都只做一个短暂的逗留，目的何在，却无从知道，尽管有时自以为对此若有所感。但是，不必深思，只要从日常生活就可以明白：人是为别人而生存的——首先是为那样一些人，我们的幸福全部依赖于他们的喜悦和健康；其次是为许多我们所不认识的人，他们的命运通过同情的纽带同我们密切结合在一起。我每天上百次地提醒自己：我的精神生活和物质生活都是以别人（包括生者和死者）的劳动为基础的，我必须尽力以同样的分量来回报我所领受了的和至今还在领受着的东西。我强烈向往俭朴的生活，时常发觉自己占用了同胞的过多劳动。我认为阶级的区分是不合理的，它最后所凭借的是暴力。我也相信，简单淳朴的生活，无论在身体上还是在精神上，对每个人都是有益的。

我完全不相信人类会有那种哲学意义上的自由。每一

Everybody acts not only under external **compulsion** but also in accordance with inner necessity. Schopenhauer's saying, "A man can do what he wants, but not want what he wants," has been a very real **inspiration** to me since my youth; it has been a continual **consolation** in the face of life's hardships, my own and others and an unfailing well-spring of tolerance. This realization mercifully **mitigates** the easily paralyzing sense of responsibility and prevents us from taking ourselves and other people all too seriously; it is conducive to a view of life which, in particular, gives humor its due.

To inquire after the meaning or object of one's own existence or that of all creatures has always seemed to me absurd from an objective point of view. And yet everybody has certain ideals which determine the direction of his **endeavors** and his judgments. In this sense I have never looked upon ease and happiness as ends in themselves—this ethical basis I call the ideal of a pigsty. The ideals which have lighted my way, and time after time have given me new courage to face life cheerfully, have been Kindness, Beauty, and Truth. Without the sense of kinship with men of like mind, without the occupation with the objective world, the eternally

个人的行为不仅受着外界的强制，而且要适应内在的必然。叔本华说："人虽然能够做他所想做的，但不能要他所想要的。"这句格言从我青年时代起就给了我真正的启示。在我自己和别人的生活面临困难的时候，它使我们得到安慰，并且是宽容持续不断的源泉。这种体会可以宽大为怀地减轻那种容易使人气馁的责任感，也可以防止我们过于严肃地对待自己和别人。以此建立的人生观特地给幽默以应有的地位。

要追究一个人自己或一切生物生存的意义或目的，从客观的观点看来，我总觉得是愚蠢可笑的。可是每个人都有一些理想，这些理想决定着他的努力和判断的方向。在这个意义上，我从来不把安逸和享乐看作生活目的本身——我把这种伦理基础叫作猪栏的理想。照亮我的道路，是善、美和真。要是没有志同道合者之间的亲切感情，要不是全神贯注于客观世界——那个在艺术和科学工作领域里永远达不到的对象，那么在我看来，生活就是空虚的。我总觉得，人们努力追求的庸俗目标——财产、虚荣、奢侈的生活——都是可

The World As I See It
我的世界观

unattainable in the field of art and scientific endeavors, life would have seemed to me empty. The trite objects of human efforts—possessions, outward success, luxury—have always seemed to me contemptible.

My passionate sense of social justice and social responsibility has always contrasted oddly with my pronounced lack of need for direct contact with other human beings and human communities. I am truly a "lone traveler" and have never belonged to my country, my home, my friend, or even my immediate family, with my whole heart; in the face of all these ties, I have never lost a sense of distance and a need for **solitude**—feelings which increase with the years. One becomes sharply aware, but without regret, of the limits of mutual understanding and consonance with other people. No doubt, such a person loses some of his innocence and unconcern; on the other hand, he is largely independent of the opinions, habits and judgments of his fellows and avoids the temptation to build his inner **equilibrium** upon such insecure foundations.

鄙的。

我有强烈的社会正义感和社会责任感，但我又明显地缺乏与别人和社会直接接触的需求，这两者总是形成古怪的对照。我实在是一个"孤独的旅客"，我未曾全心全意地属于我的国家、我的家庭、我的朋友，甚至我最为接近的亲人；在所有这些关系面前，我总是感到有一定距离而且需要保持孤独——而这种感受正与年俱增。人们会清楚地发觉，同别人的相互了解和协调一致是有限度的，但这不值得惋惜。无疑，这样的人在某种程度上会失去他的天真无邪和无忧无虑的心境。但另一方面，他却能够在很大程度上不为别人的意见、习惯和判断所左右，并且能够避免那种把他的内心平衡建立在这样一些不可靠的基础之上的诱惑。

单词解析 Word Analysis

mortal ['mɔːt(ə)l] *n.* 人类，凡人

例 Or else he would forego his mortal nature.
不然他就失去了凡人的本性。

sojourn ['sɒdʒɜːn] *n.* 逗留；旅居

例 This year's plan: a week-long sojourn to Bali in November, complete with surfing lessons.
今年的计划是11月份去巴厘岛居住一周时间，完成冲浪课程。

oppressively [ə'presɪvli] *adv.* 压迫地；沉重地

例 It was oppressively hot in the office.
办公室里热得让人感到压抑。

distinction [dɪ'stɪŋ(k)ʃ(ə)n] *n.* 区别；差别；特性；荣誉、勋章

例 That was a highly statistically significant distinction.
这是数字统计上的明显区别。

unjustified [ʌn'dʒʌstɪfaɪd] *adj.* 不正当的；未被证明其正确的

例 This smacks of unjustified optimism.
这其中有不合理的乐观意味。

philosophical [fɪlə'sɒfɪk(ə)l] *adj.* 哲学的（等于 philosophic）；冷静的

例 I especially appreciate his philosophical simplicity.
我特别欣赏他的朴素哲学。

compulsion [kəm'pʌlʃ(ə)n] *n.* 强制；强迫；强制力

例 How can compulsion serve as an ally?
强迫性冲动怎样才能变成我们的盟友？

inspiration [ɪnspɪ'reɪʃ(ə)n] *n.* 灵感；鼓舞；吸气；妙计

例 Instead, they found inspiration from reality tv competitions like *American Idol*.
相反，他们从《美国偶像》（*American Idol*）这类电视真人秀节目中找到了灵感。

consolation [ˌkɒnsəˈleɪʃ(ə)n] *n.* 安慰；慰问；起安慰作用的人或事物

例 Mr. Obama will find no consolation on the world stage.
奥巴马在国际舞台上也寻求不到安慰。

mitigate [ˈmɪtɪgeɪt] *vt.* 使缓和，使减轻

例 What could you do to mitigate the fallout?
你能做些什么来减轻受到的影响呢？

endeavor [ɪnˈdɛvə] *n.* 努力；尽力

例 The result: innovation is "an active endeavor," the authors write.
研究的结论是：创新是"积极的努力"。

passionate [ˈpæʃənət] *adj.* 热烈的；激昂的；易怒的；易被情欲所支配的

例 Mahler was also known for his passionate involvements outside marriage.
马勒也因为其轰轰烈烈的婚外情而出名。

solitude [ˈsɒlɪtjuːd] *adj.* 单独，孤独；偏僻处，隐居处

例 The motif of these volumes is that "solitude is the richness of the soul, loneliness is its poverty."
这几卷的主题是"孤独是灵魂的财富，寂寞是灵魂的贫瘠"。

equilibrium [ˌiːkwɪˈlɪbrɪəm,ekwɪ-] *n.* 均衡；平静；保持平衡的能力

例 Homeostasis is our body's attempt to maintain equilibrium.
平衡是我们的身体想要保持的状态。

语法知识点 *Grammar points*

① How strange is the lot of us mortals!

本句为how引导的感叹句。这类句子的构成一般为how+adj.+主语+谓语，也可以是how+adj.+a/an+主语+谓语。此外，在本句中us和mortal都表示"人类"，在语法上mortal为us的同位语。

另外，感叹句也可以用what引导，这类句子的构成一般为what+a/an+adj.+可数名词单数+主语+谓语，也可以是what+adj.+可数名词复数/不可数名词+主语+谓语，例如：

例 What a nice present it is!
它是一件多么好的礼物啊!

② **A man can do what he wants, but not want what he wants.**

本句为典型的宾语从句。逗号前面一句话中，do为先行词，what为引导宾语从句的关系代词；同样地，在逗号后面一句话中，want为先行词，what为引导宾语从句的关系代词。

关于宾语从句，无论主句是陈述句还是疑问句，宾语从句都必须使用陈述语序，即"主句＋连词＋宾语从句（主语＋谓语＋……）"句式。根据连接词在从句中所担任的不同成分，可分为以下四种：

1）连接词＋谓语。连接词在从句中做主语。常见的连接词有：who，what，which等。

例 Could you tell me who knows the answer, please?
你能告诉我谁知道答案吗？

2）连接词＋名词＋谓语。连接词在从句中做主语的定语。常见的连接词有：whose，what，which，how many，how much等。

例 He asked whose handwriting was the best in our class.
他问我们班上谁的书法最好。

3）连接词＋主语＋谓语。连接词在从句中做宾语、状语或表语。常见的连接词有：who (m)，what，which，how many，how much，when，why，how，where，if / whether（在句中不充当任何成分）等。

例 He hasn't decided if he'll go on a trip to Wuxi.
他还没决定是否去无锡旅行。

4）连接词＋名词＋主语＋谓语。连接词在从句中做宾语或表语的定语。常见的连接词有：what，which，how many，how much，how等。

例 Do you know which class he is in?
你知道他在哪个班吗？

经典名句 *Famous Classics*

1. Solitude is the richness of the soul, loneliness is its poverty.
   孤独是灵魂的财富，寂寞是灵魂的贫瘠。

2. But be not afraid of greatness: some men are born great, some achieve greatness, and some have greatness thrust upon them.

The World As I See It
我的世界观

不要害怕伟大：有些人生来就伟大，有些人通过努力达到伟大，有些人则不得不变得伟大。

3. An adventure is only an inconvenience rightly considered. An inconvenience is only an adventure wrongly considered.
正确地认识你的麻烦，它就成了一场冒险。如果你不能正视一场冒险，它就变成了一堆麻烦。

4. Hold it the greatest wrong to prefer life to honor and for the sake of life to lose the reason for living.
要记住，为了生存而放弃尊严，为了生存而放弃生存的意义，是最为错误的举动。

5. I postpone death by living, by suffering, by error, by risking, by giving.
我用生活、痛苦、错误、冒险与奉献——来拖延死亡。

05 Old Shoes, Happy Life
旧鞋子也有温暖

People often drop into a **gloomy** life and are unable to **extricate** themselves.

There once was a poor and frustrated salesman complaining every day that there was no platform for him to display his ability and the fate was often pulling his legs.

At Christmas Eve, every family decorated their houses with lanterns and streamers and it was very **festive** everywhere. But he was **alone** sitting in a bench in a park and recalling the past. It was on the same day last year when he was also alone drinking his Christmas day away, without new clothes, new shoes, let alone a new car and a new house.

"Damn! I have to spend this Christmas day with these old shoes again." he signed and began to take off the old shoes. Suddenly, he glanced a young man in a wheel chair passing by him with his hands **arduously** pushing the wheel forward. It **dawned** on him that he was so lucky to have shoes to wear while that man did not even have the chance. Afterwards, the sales man did anything with a calm mood and cherished every opportunity

人常常会陷于幽暗的人生胡同不能自拔。

有个生活比较潦倒的销售员，每天都埋怨自己怀才不遇，命运在捉弄他。

圣诞节前夕，家家户户张灯结彩，充满佳节的热闹气氛。他坐在公园里的一张椅子上，开始回顾往事。去年的今天，他也是孤单一人，以醉酒度过他的圣诞节，没有新衣，没有新鞋，更甭谈新车子、新房子。

"唉，今年我又要穿着这双旧鞋子度过圣诞节了！"说着准备脱掉这旧鞋子。这时候，他突然看见一个年轻人自己滑着轮椅从他身边路过。他顿悟："我有鞋子穿是多么幸福！他连穿鞋子的机会都没有啊！"之后，推销员做任何一件事都心平气和，珍惜机会，发奋图强，力争上游。数年之后，他终于改变了自己的生活，成了一名百万富翁。

环顾四周，我们会发觉社会上有许多天生残缺的人，他们对生活充满信心，从不抱怨

to improve himself. He worked hard and tried his best to make a progress every day. Several years later, he **eventually** changed his life totally and became a millionaire.

If you look all around, you will find there are so many people who were born disabled in the society but they are confident in life and never complain about the unfair **destiny**. They are also not to beg others' **almsgiving**. Instead, they constantly strive to make themselves stronger and more excellent to serve the society. By contrast, we should feel ashamed. We are born healthy, but we are fed up with life; we complain about our colleagues and dissatisfy with our jobs.

Maybe all of us would feel afraid when we realize we have fallen into such frustrating state of life, but worse is you even do not realize you have fallen into such a **jeopardous** situation.

上天对他们的不公平，也不乞求他人救济，反而自立自强，脱颖而出，成为有用之才。与他们相比，我们会觉得很惭愧，我们生来五官端正，手脚齐全，却为何厌倦生活厌倦人生，抱怨同事，不满意自己的工作。

也许我们每个人对陷入这种幽暗的人生胡同都感到可怕，但更可怕的是，当你陷入这种危险的境地却浑然不知。

单词解析 Word Analysis

gloomy ['glu:mi] *adj* 黑暗的；沮丧的；阴郁的

例 Inside it's gloomy after all that sunshine.
尽管阳光明媚，里面依然暗淡无光。

例 Miller is gloomy about the fate of the serious playwright in America.
米勒对这位严肃剧作家在美国的命运颇为忧虑。

extricate ['ekstrikeit] *v.* 使解脱；解救；使游离

例 He endeavoured to extricate the car, digging with his hands in the blazing sunshine.
他在烈日下用手挖着，拼命想要把那辆汽车弄出来。

festive ['festiv] *adj.* 欢乐的；喜庆的；节日的

例 The Captain's Party on Saturday evening is the cruise's most festive event.
周六晚上的船长晚会是游轮上最喜庆的活动。

alone [ə'ləʊn] *adv.* 单独地，独自地；孤苦伶仃的，无依无靠的

例 I couldn't imagine why he would want to be alone with me.
我想象不出为什么他会想和我独处。

例 Never in her life had she felt so alone, so abandoned.
她一生中从来没有感到如此孤单，如此无助。

arduously ['ɑːdʒʊəsli] *adv.* 严酷地；费力地

例 He arduously and soon began to play in local bands.
他拼命学习弹奏，很快就加入了当地的一个乐队。

dawn [dɔːn] *v.* 被领悟；破晓；出现

例 A new era seemed to be about to dawn for the coach and his young team.
对于那名教练和他的年轻球队来说，一个崭新的时代似乎即将到来。

eventually [ɪ'ventʃʊəli] *adv.* 终于，最后；竟；总归；终究

例 Eventually, the water will permeate through the surrounding concrete.
最终，水会渗透进周围的混凝土中。

destiny ['destəni] *n.* 命运，定数，天命

例 We are masters of our own destiny.
我们是自己命运的主宰者。

almsgiving [ɑːmz'gɪvɪŋ] *n.* 救济，施舍

例 True charity does not consist in almsgiving.
真正的仁慈并不在于施舍。

Old Shoes, Happy Life
旧鞋子也有温暖 05

jeopardous [ˈdʒepədəs] *adj.* 冒险的

例 Hot money is jeopardous to the balance of international payment the stability of RMB exchange rate.
"热钱"不利于国际收支平衡和人民币汇率稳定。

语法知识点 Grammar points

① People often drop into a gloomy life and are unable to extricate themselves.

drop into 不知不觉变得；顺便进入；偶然进入

例 You can't drop out of school and just drop into a good job.
你不可能在退学后就有一个好的工作在等你。

② But he was alone sitting in a bench in a park and recalling the past. It was on the same day last year when he was also alone drinking his Christmas day away, without new clothes, new shoes, let alone a new car and a new house.

let alone 更不必说，不干涉，不打扰

例 If a difference is going to be made in this world, let alone in your own life, it is up to you.
如果这个世界正在发生改变，那就更不用提你自己的生活了，而这种改变是由你来决定。

例 Let her alone when she is not happy.
她不高兴时别去惹她。

alone 独自的，单独的 lonely 寂寞的，孤寂的

例 He is alone, but he doesn't feel lonely.
他独自一人，但并不感到寂寞。

③ "Damn! I have to spend this Christmas day with these old shoes again." he signed and began to take off the old shoes.

take off 脱掉；（飞机）起飞；（产品、活动、事业等）腾飞，突然成功

例 We eventually took off at 11 o'clock and arrived in Venice at 1.30.
我们终于在11点起飞，1:30 到达威尼斯。

In 1944, he met Edith Piaf, and his career took off.
1944 年，他结识了伊迪思·比阿夫，从此他的事业开始腾飞。

④ It dawned on him that he was so lucky to have shoes to wear while that man did not even have the chance.

此句中while译为"却，而"，用于强调两种情况、活动等之间的差别

例 That region has plenty of natural resources while this one has none.
那个地区自然资源丰富，这个地区却一点也没有。

⑤ We are born healthy, but we are fed up with life; we complain about our colleagues and dissatisfy with our jobs.

be fed up with 极厌倦；吃得过饱

例 People will be fed up with you if you have a hard head.
如果你为人老是那样，人家很快就会讨厌你的。

经典名句 Famous Classics

1. The humorous man recognizes that absolute purity, absolute justice, absolute logic and perfection are beyond human achievement and that men have been able to live happily for thousands of years in a state of genial frailty.
有幽默感的人明白，绝对的纯净、绝对的公平、绝对的逻辑以及完美是人类无法企及的，人类在平凡与脆弱中，已经欣然存活了上万年。

2. Life is the greatest bargain; we get it for nothing.
生命是一笔再划算不过的交易；我们免费得到了它。

3. Death, my son, is a benefit for all of us, it is the night of this turbulent day that we call Life.
死亡，我的孩子，对我们来说都有好处，在我们奔波的白天终于结束

时，死亡是得以歇息的夜晚。

4. Electric communication will never be a substitute for the face of someone who with their soul encourages another person to be brave and true.
电子通信永远无法代替人们面对面的交流，无法代替一个能带来勇气和真诚的灵魂。

5. Friendship is a disinterested commerce between equals; love, an abject intercourse between tyrants and slaves.
友谊是平等的人们之间无利益纠葛的来往；而爱情总是发号施令的一方与被奴役的一方之间可悲的交易。

6. An open foe may prove a curse, but a pretended friend is worse.
虽然你公开的敌人会咒骂并加害于你，但是假装是你的朋友的人更加可怕。

7. You shall judge of a man by his foes as well as by his friends.
要评价一个人，既要看他的朋友，也要看他的敌人。

8. Friendship is unnecessary, like philosophy, like art. It has no survival value; rather it is one of those things that give value to survival.
如同哲学、艺术一样，友谊也不是必需品。它没有生存价值，然而它是能够给人们的生存带来价值的东西之一。

9. It is important to our friends to believe that we are unreservedly frank with them, and important to friendship that we are not.
对朋友们来说，知道我们对他们坦诚以待是非常重要的；而对友谊来说，同样重要的是，不要真的对他们事事相告。

10. He who has a thousand friends has not a friend to spare, and he who has one enemy will meet him everywhere.
一个人就算有上千个朋友也不算多，而就算他只有一个敌人，也会到处碰到这个敌人。

06 A Lesson of Life
生活的一课

"Everything happens for the best," my mother said whenever I faced disappointment. "If you carry on, one day something good will happen. And you'll realize that it wouldn't have happened if not for that previous disappointment."

Mother was right, as I discovered after graduating from college in 1932, I had decided to try for a job in radio, then work my way up to sports announcer. I **hitchhiked** to Chicago and knocked on the door of every station—and got turned down every time. In one **studio**, a kind lady told me that big stations couldn't risk hiring an inexperienced person. "Go out in the sticks and find a small station that'll give you a chance," she said. I **thumbed** home to Dixon, Illinois.

While there were no radio—announcing jobs in Dixon, my father said Montgomery Ward had opened a store and wanted a local **athlete** to manage its sports department. Since Dixon was where I had played high school football, I applied. The job sounded just right for me. But I wasn't

"一切都会好的。"每当我遇到挫折时，母亲就会说："如果你坚持下去，总要一天会有好事发生。如果没有以前的挫折，就不会有现在的一切。"

母亲是对的，发现这个是在1932年，我刚从大学毕业。我已决定试着在电台找个事儿做，然后争取做体育节目的播音员。我搭便车到了芝加哥，挨个电台地敲门推销自己——但每次都被拒绝了。在一个播音室里，一位好心的女士告诉我，大的广播电台是不会冒险雇用没经验的新手的。我搭车回到我的家乡，那是伊利诺伊州的迪克森。

在迪克森当时还没有电台播音员这样的工作，父亲说，蒙哥马利·沃德开了一家新商店，想雇请一个本地的运动员管理店里的体育部。我中学时曾在迪克森打过橄榄球，出于这个原因我去申请了这份工作。工作听起来挺适合我的，但是我没被聘用。

我的沮丧心情一定表现出

A Lesson of Life
生活的一课

hired.

My disappointment must have shown. "Everything happens for the best." Mom reminded me. Dad offered me the car to hunt job. I tried WOC Radio in Davenport, Iowa. The program director, a wonderful Scotsman named Peter MacArthur told me they had already hired an **announcer**.

As I left his office, my **frustration** boiled over. I asked aloud, "How can a **fellow** get to be a sports announcer if he can't get a job in a radio station." I was waiting for the elevator when I heard MacArthur calling, "What was that you said about sports? Do you know anything about football?" Then he stood me before a microphone and asked me broadcast an **imaginary** game.

On my way home, as I have many times since, I thought of my mother's words, "If you carry on, one day something good will happen. Something wouldn't have happened if not for that previous disappointment."

I often wonder what direction my life might have taken if I'd not gotten the job at Montgomery Ward.

来了。母亲提醒我："一切都会好的！"爸爸给我买了一辆汽车找工作。我试着到爱荷华州达文波特的WOC电台去求职。那里的电台节目总监是一个很棒的苏格兰人，名叫彼得·麦克阿瑟，他告诉我他们已经雇到播音员了。

离开他办公室时，我的挫折感达到了极点。我大声地说："一个连在电台都找不到工作的家伙又怎么能成为体育节目的播音员呢？"等电梯时，我听到麦克阿瑟喊道："你说什么体育？你懂橄榄球吗？"接着他让我站到麦克风前面，请我解说一场想象中的比赛。

在回家的路上——以后也有很多次的，我思考着母亲的那句话："如果你坚持下去，总要一天会有好事发生。如果没有以前的挫折，就不会有现在的一切。"

我常想，如果当年我得到蒙哥马利·沃德的那份工作，我的人生之路又会怎样走呢？

单词解析 Word Analysis

hitchhike ['hɪtʃhaɪk] v. 搭便车

例 Two men hitchhike towards Los Angeles a 1937 photo.
1937年，两个想搭便车到洛杉矶的男人。

studio ['stjuːdiəʊ] n. 工作室；演播室；画室；电影制片厂

例 The studio is midway between his aunt's old home and his cottage.
工作室就在从他姑姑的老宅到他的小屋的途中。

thumb [θʌm] v. 以拇指拨弄；做搭车手势；笨拙地摆弄；翻阅

例 It may interest you to know that a boy answering Rory's description thumbed a ride to Howth.
你或许会对这个消息感兴趣，有个和罗里描述的一模一样的小男孩搭便车到了霍斯。

athlete ['æθliːt] n. 运动员，体育家；身强力壮的人

例 I was no athlete.
我根本不是当运动员的料。

announcer [əˈnaʊnsə(r)] n. 广播员；宣告者

例 A radio announcer may have an audience of millions.
一个广播员可能拥有数百万名听众。

frustration [frʌˈstreɪʃn] n. 挫折；失败；挫败；失意

例 Sometimes frustration and anger can boil over into direct and violent action.
有时挫折和愤怒会以直接的暴力形式爆发出来。

fellow ['feləʊ] n. 家伙；朋友；同事；会员

例 He stood out in terms of competence from all his fellows.
他在能力上远远胜过其他同事。

imaginary [ɪˈmædʒɪnəri] adj. 想象的；虚构的，假想的

例 Lots of children have imaginary friends.
许多孩子都会凭空想象一些朋友。

A Lesson of Life
生活的一课

语法知识点 *Grammar points*

① **Mother was right, as I discovered after graduating from college in 1932, I had decided to try for a job in radio, then work my way up to sports announcer.**

work one's way up to 努力成为/做到……

例 He has worked his way up from junior clerk to managing director.
他从初级职员升到总经理。

② **While there were no radio—announcing jobs in Dixon, my father said Montgomery Ward had opened a store and wanted a local athlete to manage its sports department.**

通常情况下while和when的意思一样："当……时候"，但while在该句话中为连词，意为"然而"。

例 The two ministers have yet to meet, but may do so while in New York.
两位部长尚未会面，但可能会在纽约碰头。

The first two services are free, while the third costs £35.00.
前两项服务免费，但是第三项服务要花35英镑。

③ **I was waiting for the elevator when I heard MacArthur calling, "What was that you said about sports? Do you know anything about football?"**

when引导时间状语从句，表示"当……的时候"，when既可以指时间段，也可指时间点，从句中既可用延续性动词，也可用非延续性动词，且动作既可和主句的动作同时发生，又可在主句的动作之前或之后发生。

例 When the decision was read out Mrs. Gardner thanked the judges.
判决书宣读完，加德纳夫人向法官们表示感谢。

例 When the wind blows, all the doors rattle.
只要风一吹，这门就吱嘎作响。

035

经典名句 Famous Classics

1. The greatest test of courage on earth is to bear defeat without losing heart.
   世界上对勇气的最大考验是忍受失败而不丧失信心。

2. A man's best friends are his ten fingers.
   人最好的朋友是自己的十个手指。

3. Only they who fulfill their duties in everyday matters will fulfill them on great occasions.
   只有在日常生活中尽责的人才会在重大时刻尽责。

4. The reason why a great man is great is that he resolves to be a great man.
   伟人之所以伟大，是因为他立志要成为伟大的人。

5. Suffering is the most powerful teacher of life.
   苦难是人生最伟大的老师。

6. Death comes to all, but great achievements raise a monument which shall endure until the sun grows old.
   死亡无人能免，但非凡的成就会树起一座纪念碑，它将一直立到太阳冷却之时。

7. The world is like a mirror: Frown at it and it frowns at you; smile, and it smiles too.
   世界犹如一面镜子：朝它皱眉它就朝你皱眉，朝它微笑它也朝你微笑。

8. There's only one corner of the universe you can be sure of improving, and that's your own self.
   这个宇宙中只有一个角落你肯定可以改进，那就是你自己。

9. One never lose anything by politeness.
   讲礼貌不吃亏。

10. The shortest way to do many things is to do only one thing at a time.
    做许多事情的捷径就是一次只做一件事。

07 Keep Your Fork
紧握餐叉

There was a woman who had been **diagnosed** with a **terminal** illness and was given three months to live. So as she began getting her things "in order", she asked for her **pastor** to come to her house to discuss certain aspects of her final wishes. She told him which songs she wanted sung at the service and what dress she wanted to be buried in. Everything was in order and as the pastor was preparing to leave, the woman suddenly remembered one final request, "Please, Pastor, just one more thing," she said **excitedly**. "This is very important to me," the woman continued, "I want to be buried holding a fork in my right hand."

The pastor **gazed** at the woman, at a loss for words. "That surprises you, doesn't it?" the woman asked. The pastor replied, "Well, to be quite honest, I am puzzled by the request." The woman explained, "You see, Pastor, in all my years of attending church socials, I remember that when the dishes were being cleared after the main course, someone would **inevitably** lean over to me and say, 'Keep your fork.' It was my

有一位女士被诊断出疾病到了晚期，只剩三个月的时间。当她开始安排后事的时候，她把牧师叫到家里商量她的遗愿。她告诉牧师在葬礼上她想要什么音乐，穿什么衣服。所有事情都安排好了，当牧师准备离开的时候，她又突然想到最后的一个要求，"牧师，请听我说最后一件事。"她兴奋地说，"这对我非常重要。在我被埋葬的时候我想右手拿一把餐叉。"

牧师凝视着她，不知该说什么。她问："听到我这么说，你很吃惊，对吧？"牧师回答道："老实说，我挺迷惑的。"她解释道："牧师，你知道，这些年我参加教堂活动，我记得在上了主菜之后餐具会被清理，有人会走过来弯腰对我说，'拿好您的餐叉。'这是一餐中我最喜欢的部分，因为我知道更好的将要到来。一餐中最好的东西会放在最后！"牧师专心地听着，他的脸上浮现出一丝微笑。她继续说道："所以我想让人们

037

favorite part of the meal because I knew that something better was coming."

"Something wonderful was to end the meal!" The pastor listened **intently** and a smile came upon his face. The woman continued, "So, I just want people to see me there with a fork in my hand and I want them to wonder... 'What's with the for'... then I want you to tell them, 'Keep your fork... the best is yet to come.'" She knew and trusted that the best was yet to come.

At the **funeral**, every one that walked by the woman's coffin saw her wearing a beautiful dress with her favorite Bible held in her left hand and a fork held in her right hand. Over and over the pastor heard people ask the question, "Why is she holding a fork?" and his smile began to get larger and brighter each time. During his message, the pastor explained the fork and what it **symbolized** to her. So the next time you reach for your fork, let it remind you, oh, so gently, that the best is yet to come.

看到我躺在那里，手里拿着一把叉子，他们会想要知道'餐叉是用来做什么的呢？'，然后我想让你告诉他们：'拿好你们的餐叉，最好的就要来了。'"她知道，并且坚信最好的就要来了。

在葬礼上，每个经过这位女士棺材的人都看到她穿着一条漂亮的裙子，左手拿着她最爱的圣经，右手拿着一把餐叉。牧师听到人们一遍又一遍地问那个问题："为什么她要拿一把餐叉？"每次听到，牧师都会变得更开心。在祷告的时候，牧师解释了餐叉对她的意义。因此，下次你拿到餐叉的时候，让它轻轻地提醒你，最好的就要来了。

单词解析 Word Analysis

diagnose [ˌdaɪəɡˈnoʊs] v. 判断；诊断（疾病）

例 Geological investigations must correctly diagnose a specific soil-like condition.

Keep Your Fork 07 紧握餐叉

地质调查必须正确地判断出特殊的土状条件。

terminal [ˈtɜːrmɪnl] *adj.* 末端的；终点的；晚期的；（每）学期的
例 About 70% patients were in terminal as they are diagnosed.
在确诊时约有70%的病人为中晚期。

pastor [ˈpæstər] *n.* 牧师
例 The villagers all loved the kind pastor.
村民们都爱戴这个好心的牧师。

excitedly [ɪkˈsaɪtɪdlɪ] *adv.* 兴奋地，激动地；勃然；兴冲冲
例 I was so excited when I went to sign the paperwork I could hardly write.
去签文件时我非常兴奋，几乎无法写字。

gaze [ɡeɪz] *v.* 凝视
例 She sat gazing out of the window.
她坐着凝视着窗外。

inevitably [ɪnˈevɪtəblɪ] *adv.* 不可避免地
例 The decision will inevitably cut both ways.
这个决定不可避免地产生两种结果。

intently [ɪnˈtentlɪ] *adv.* 一心一意地；心无旁骛地；专心地
例 She regarded him closely, intently, curiously, etc.
她紧紧地、目不转睛地、好奇地注视着他。

funeral [ˈfjuːnərəl] *n.* 葬礼，丧礼；后果由……自负（习语）
例 His funeral will be on Thursday at Blackburn Cathedral.
他的葬礼将于星期四在布莱克本大教堂举行。
None of my business, I guess. It's your funeral.
我想是不关我什么事儿，你就自寻死路吧。

symbolize [ˈsɪmbəlaɪz] *v.* 象征；用记号表现
例 Easter eggs symbolize the renewal of life.
复活蛋象征新生。

语法知识点 *Grammar points*

① There was a woman who had been diagnosed with a terminal illness and was given three months to live.

这个句子是一个who引导的定语从句，先行词是a woman，who在从句中充当主语。

be diagnosed with 被诊断出患有……

> 例 He has recently been diagnosed with angina.
> 他最近被诊断出患有心绞痛。

② She told him which songs she wanted sung at the service and what dress she wanted to be buried in.

这个句子是which和what引导的宾语从句。

be buried in 被埋葬

> 例 What has happened shall be buried in oblivion.
> 既往不咎。
>
> Those dead soldiers were buried in the tombs.
> 那些死去的战士被埋葬在坟墓里。

③ The pastor gazed at the woman, at a loss for words.

gaze at 凝视，注视

> 例 He gazed at the scene with staring eyes.
> 他瞪大眼睛注视着这场面。
>
> For some time, she gazed at a pair of fur-lined high boots on display.
> 她盯着陈列在橱窗里的一双有毛皮里子的长筒靴子看了好一会儿。

at a loss 困惑；不知所措；亏本地

> 例 He is always at a loss what to say in front of strangers.
> 他在生人面前总是不知要说什么。
>
> He was quite at a loss for words of consolation.
> 他简直想不出安慰的话来。
>
> He was at a loss for a suitable reply.
> 他不知所措，找不出合适的答复。

Keep Your Fork 紧握餐叉 07

④ **I remember that when the dishes were being cleared after the main course, someone would inevitably lean over to me and say, "Keep your fork".**

这个句子是一个宾语从句，从句部分做remember的宾语。宾语从句中还包含了一个when引导的时间状语从句。

lean over to 向某处倾斜，向某人、某方向弯腰

例 Fatso leaned over to whisper in her ear.
胖子欠身对她耳语几句。

The damaged ship was leaning over to port.
损坏的船向左舷倾斜。

⑤ **At the funeral, every one that walked by the woman's coffin saw her wearing a beautiful dress with her favorite Bible held in her left hand and a fork held in her right hand.**

every one做先行词，that引导了定语从句，that在从句中做主语。
at the funeral 在葬礼上（注意at的使用）
相同的用法还有：at the party在聚会上；at the meeting 在会上

例 His behavior at the party was most regrettable.
他在宴会上的作为令人深感遗憾。

The question is bound to come up at the meeting.
会上必然要讨论这个问题。

see sb. doing 看见某人正在做某事

例 We saw him working in the garden this morning.
我们看见他今早在花园里干活。

经典名句 Famous Classics

1. Without wearing any mask we are conscious of, we have a special face for each friend.
我们无意识地戴着面具在生活，而对每一个朋友，我们都戴上不同的面具。

2. To conceal anything from those to whom I am attached, is not in my nature. I can never close my lips where I have opened my

heart.

我无法对自己所爱的人隐瞒任何事情,这是天性使然。当我打开心扉的时候,我也无法闭口不言。

3. No one is useless in this world who lightens the burden of it to anyone else.
   如果一个人能够为别人减轻负担,他在这个世界上就是有用的。

4. To help a friend in need is easy, but to give him your time is not always opportune.
   帮助有困难的朋友很简单,但我们却总是没有时间。

5. We all want to help one another. Human beings are like that. We want to live by each other's happiness, not by each other's misery.
   我们都想要互相帮助,人类生性如此。我们要生活在彼此的快乐之中,而非痛苦之中。

6. Whatever you think of your friend, he thinks the same of you.
   你怎么看待自己的朋友,他们也会这样看待你。

读书笔记

08 The Enchantment of Creeks
小溪的魅力

Nearly everybody has a creek in his past, a confiding waterway that rose in the spring of youth.

My creek wound between Grandfather's **apricot** orchard and a neighbor's hillside **pasture**. Its banks were **shaded** by cottonwoods and redwood trees and a thick tangle of blackberries and wild **grapevines**. On hot summer days the quiet water flowed clear and cold over gravel bars where I fished for **trout**.

Nothing historic ever happens in these recollected creeks. But their persistence in memory suggests that creeks are bigger than they seem, more like a part of our hearts and minds than mighty rivers.

Creek time is measured in the lives of strange creatures, in sand flecked **caddis** worms under the rocks, sudden **gossamer** clouds of mayflies in the afternoon, or **minnows** of darting like silvers of inspiration into the dimness of creek fate. Mysteries float in creeks' **riffles**, crawl over their **pebbled** bottoms and slink under the roots of trees.

While rivers are heavy with

几乎每一个人的过去都流淌着一条小溪，它发源于少年时代，一路潺潺絮语而来。

我心中的小溪蜿蜒流淌在祖父的杏树园和邻居的山腰的草地之间。三角叶杨和红杉将两岸遮得严严实实，黑刺莓和野葡萄盘根错节，密不透风。在炎热的夏天，安静的水流清澈清凉，流过我钓鳟鱼的地方。

这些忆旧的小溪没发生过什么历史性的事情。但是它们顽强的记忆表明，这些小溪比它们看起来的要大，比大河更像我们心灵和思想的一部分。

小溪的时间由奇奇怪怪的生命组成：岩石下钻在沙子里的鱼虫，下午突然出现的成群的蜉蝣，飞奔的米诺鱼像银色的气息渗入小溪暗淡的命运。神秘的东西漂过浅滩，爬过铺满鹅卵石的河床，潜入树根底下。

大河由于复杂性和沉淀而显沉重，小溪则清澈、纯净、活泼，充满了梦想和希望。无须父母的担心，孩子们就可以涉水而过。他们可以独自去小溪，在水中捉小虾，在岸边

sophistication and **sediment**, creeks are clear, innocent, **boisterous**, full of dream and promise. A child can wade across them without a parent's cautions. You can go it alone, jig for crayfish, swing from ropes along the bank. Creeks belong to childhood, drawing you into the wider world, teaching you the curve of the earth.

Above all, a creek offers the mind a chance to penetrate the alien universe of water, of tadpoles and trout. What drifts in creek water is the possibility of other worlds inside and above our own. Poet Robert Frost wrote: "It flows between us, over us, and with us. And it is time, strength, tone, light, life and love."

Creeks lead one on, like perfume on the wind. A creek is something that disappears around a bend, into the ground, into the next dimension. To follow a creek is to seek new acquaintance with life.

I still find myself following creeks. In high mountain meadows I'll trace their course into the lime green grass and deep glacial duff, marveling at the sparkle of quartz and mica. The pursuit liquefies my citified haste and lifts weight from my shoulders. Once, in the California desert, as hummingbirds darted from cactus blossoms, I heard the babble of rushing water. My ears led me

系上绳子荡秋千。小溪属于童年，将孩子们带入一个更加广阔的世界，让他们领略到大地起伏的轮廓。

尤其是，小溪给了思想一个机会，去探索外星的水、蝌蚪和鳟鱼。飘荡在小溪里的是其他世界的可能性。诗人罗伯特·弗罗斯特写道："它流动着，在我们之间、超过我们或与我们同行。它是时间、是力量、是声音、是光、是生命和爱。"

小溪引航前行，像风中的香水。小溪绕一个弯就会消失不见，进入到地底下，进入到下一维度。追随一条小溪就是追寻新的生活。

我发现自己仍然追随小溪。在高山草甸，我会到绿草丛处、冰川处、闪亮的石英和云母处追寻它的踪迹。这个追求化解了我应对城市生活的匆忙，减轻了我肩膀上的重压。一次，在加州沙漠中，当蜂鸟飞离仙人掌花的时候，我听见哗啦啦的水流的声音。我的耳朵带着我穿过满是灰尘的山坡和播过种的山沟走到了令人意想不到的清澈、寒冷的水流，从岩石冲向岩石，填满了小水池。就像发现圣经一样，它使我充满了喜悦。

over dusty hillsides and sown scabrous ravines to an unexpected ribbon of clear, cold water, leaping from rock to rock, filling little pools. The discovery seemed Biblical. It filled me with joy.

单词解析 Word Analysis

apricot [ˈæprɪkɑːt] *n.* 杏子；杏色；杏树

- You have a choice of marmalade or apricot jam for breakfast.
  在用早餐时，您可选用橘子酱或杏酱。

pasture [ˈpæstʃər] *n.* 牧场；草原

- The land was used chiefly for pasture.
  这土地多半用作牧场。

shade [ʃeɪd] *v.* 遮蔽；使阴暗；使渐变；略减（价格） *n.* （色彩的）浓淡，深浅，色度

- He tried to shade in one side of his drawing.
  他想把他那幅画的一边涂成阴影。
  In the mornings the sky appeared a heavy shade of mottled gray.
  清晨，天空呈现出斑驳的深灰色。
  As the dusk shaded into night, we drove slowly through narrow alleys.
  夜幕渐渐降临，我们驱车在狭窄的胡同里缓慢前行。

grapevine [ˈɡreɪpvaɪn] *n.* 葡萄藤；葡萄树；秘密信息来源

- The grapevine creeps along the wall.
  葡萄藤沿墙蔓延。

trout [traʊt] *n.* 鳟鱼；鳟鱼肉

- I caught seven trout in fifteen minutes.
  我十五分钟内捉到七条鳟鱼。

caddis ['kædɪs] *n.* 石蚕（鱼饵）；精纺毛纱编带

例 Instead, it secretes a glue and uses this to stick bits of sand together to form its casing, in the way that a freshwater caddis larva does.
相反，它分泌胶质后，使用它与沙子一起构建自己的壳，与淡水石蛾幼虫的构建方式相同。

gossamer ['gɑːsəmər] *adj.* 薄弱的；轻飘飘的

例 The prince helped the princess, who was still in her delightful gossamer gown.
王子搀扶着仍穿着那套美丽薄纱晚礼服的公主。

minnow ['mɪnoʊ] *n.* 鲦鱼；小淡水鱼；无足轻重的小公司；不起眼的小型运动队

例 These two companies are both minnows in the international market.
在国际市场上，这两家公司都是微不足道的。

riffle ['rɪfl] *n.* 急流；涟漪；洗牌；浅滩；槽沟

例 He fished on the river riffle.
他在河流浅滩处钓鱼。

sophistication [səˌfɪstɪ'keɪʃn] *n.* 老练；精明；复杂；精密；有教养；诡辩；强词夺理

例 Despite her scruffy clothes, there was an air of sophistication about her.
尽管她衣衫褴褛，但神态老练世故。

sediment ['sedɪmənt] *n.* 沉淀物

例 If you are replacing the bottom element, remove the accumulated sediment on the bottom of the tank.
如果是替换下部元件，需要清除累积在内胆底部的沉淀物。

boisterous ['bɔɪstərəs] *adj.* 喧闹的；狂暴的

例 The infinite sky is motionless overhead and the restless water is boisterous.
头上是静止的无垠的天空，不息的海水狂暴肆虐。

语法知识点 *Grammar points*

① **But their persistence in memory suggests that creeks are bigger than they seem, more a part of our hearts and minds than mighty rivers.**

这个句子中有一个that引导的宾语从句，从句做suggests的宾语。

more than 超过；多于；不仅仅；非常

例 For safety's sake, don't drive more than 30 kilometers per hour in the city.
为了安全起见，在市内开车时速不要超过三十公里。

② **You can go it alone, jig for crayfish, swing from ropes along the bank. Creeks belong to childhood, drawing you into the wider world, teaching you the curve of the earth.**

swing from 悬挂

例 He swings from wild optimism to total despair.
他由极其乐观一下变为完全绝望。

belong to 属于；为……之一员

例 Alder trees belong to the birch family.
赤杨属于桦木科。

draw into 卷入；驶进；开到

例 They were reluctant to be drawn into the conflict.
他们不愿卷入这场冲突。

这个句子中，最后drawing you into the wider world, teaching you the curve of the earth是两个现在分词短语做伴随状语。

③ **Above all, a creek offers the mind a chance to penetrate the alien universe of water, of tadpoles and trout.**

above all 首先；尤其是

例 He longs above all (else) to see his family again.
他尤其渴望再见到家人。

offer sb. sth. 向某人提供某物

例 She offered me a seat.
她给我让了一个座。

047

④ To follow a creek is to seek new acquaintance with life.

这个句子中，前面用to do不定式，后面也要用to do不定式，保持一致。
acquaintance with 相识，了解

> I have a slight acquaintance with Japanese.
> 我略通日文。

经典名句 Famous Classics

1. The important thing in life is not the victory but the contest; the essential thing is not to have won but to have fought well.
   生活最重要的不是胜利，而是竞争本身；最关键的不是成功，而是打了一场漂亮的战役。

2. We are like sailors who must rebuild their ship on the open sea, never able to dismantle it in dry-dock and to reconstruct it there out of the best materials.
   人生就像是水手需要在海上修复他们的船只，你无法在陆地的码头上把船拆了然后用最好的材料重建。

3. I often feel, and ever more deeply I realize, that fate and character are the same conception.
   我常觉得，并且越发明白，命运和性格是两个相同的概念。

4. It's at the borders of pain and suffering that the men are separated from the boys.
   只有经过了痛苦和挣扎的边境，男人们才能脱离男孩的世界。

5. Time is the wisest counselor of all.
   时间是最高明的顾问。

6. Work is hard. Distractions are plentiful. And time is short.
   工作总是让人劳累。分心的事情总是接踵而至。时间总是太过短暂。

7. Always remember that the future comes one day at a time.
   永远记住，未来每天都在发生。

09 Sleeping Through the Storm
未雨绸缪

It was spring, in western America, the weather was getting warmer. There was a young man who went out to find a job on a farm. He came to a small farm, which belonged to an old farmer and his wife. He told the farmer he wanted to apply for a job as a **farmhand**. When the farmer asked for his **qualifications**, "What can you do, boy?" The young man said, "I can sleep when the wind blows."

This answer quite **puzzled** the farmer and his wife, but he looked honest and reliable, so the couple liking the young man decided to hire him.

Two months passed and the young man had worked well on the farm, nothing unusual.

One night, the farmer and his wife were awakened by a **violent** storm. They quickly began to check things out to see if all was secure. They found that the shutters of the farmhouse had been securely fastened. A good supply of **logs** had been set next to the fireplace.

The young man slept **soundly**.

The farmer and his wife then **inspected** their property. They found that the farm tools had been placed in the storage shed, safe from the elements. The

那是美国西部的一个春天，天气开始变暖，一个年轻人离开家，想在农场里找些活儿干。于是他来到一个小农场。这个农场的主人是一对老夫妇。年轻人告诉农场主他想在农场里当一个帮手。农场主问道："年轻人，你能干些什么？"那个年轻人回答："我能在刮风的时候睡得着觉。"

他的回答让农场主夫妇感到迷惑不解，但是他看起来诚实可靠，老两口也很喜欢这个孩子，于是就决定把他雇了下来。

两个月过去了，这个年轻人在农场里干得还不错，但也没有什么特别之处。

一天夜里，突如其来的暴风雨把睡梦中的农场主夫妇惊醒了。他们赶紧起来查看农场里的东西是否安全。他们发现农舍的门都已牢牢地拴紧。一大堆木头已经码在壁炉旁。

再看那个年轻人，他正睡得香呢。

然后，农场主夫妇检查了他们的东西，发现农具都已经收进了仓库，远离风雨。拖拉机已经开进了车库。牲口棚也

049

tractor had been moved into the garage. The barn was properly locked. Even the animals were calm. All was well.

The farmer then understood the meaning of the young man's words, "I can sleep when the wind blows." Because the farmhand did his work loyally and **faithfully** when the skies were clear, he was prepared for the storm when it broke. So when the wind blew, he was not afraid. He could sleep in peace.

锁得好好的，就连家畜也都很平静。一切正常。

这时农场主终于明白了当初这个年轻人为什么说他能在刮风的时候睡得着觉。因为这个小伙子已经在天气好的时候尽心尽力地干好了他该干的活，为暴风雨的到来做好了准备，所以当暴风雨袭来时他没什么可担心的，自然也就能高枕无忧了。

单词解析 Word Analysis

farmhand ['fɑːmhænd] *n.* 农场工人

- Before liberation, his father worked for a landlord as a farmhand.
  解放前，他的父亲给地主当长工。

qualification [ˌkwɒlɪfɪ'keɪʃn] *n.* 资格；限制；条件；赋予资格

- Lucy wants to study medicine but needs more qualifications.
  露西希望学医，但是需要通过更多的资格考试。

puzzled ['pʌzld] *adj.* 困惑的；搞糊涂的；茫然的 *v.*（puzzle的过去式）使迷惑，使难解

- Joe passed his hand over his face and looked puzzled.
  乔用手摸了一把脸，看上去疑惑不解。
  They puzzled over the question for quite a while.
  这问题他们苦苦地想了很久。

violent ['vaɪələnt] *adj.* 猛烈的；暴力的

- A violent explosion seemed to jolt the whole ground.
  剧烈的爆炸好像要把整个地面都掀起来。
  A quarter of current inmates have committed violent crimes.
  现在关押的犯人中有1/4是暴力犯罪。

log [lɒg] *n.* 航行日志；原木；记录

例 It is the original log cabin where Lincoln was born.
林肯诞生于原来那座原木小屋。
The family made an official complaint to a ship's officer, which was recorded in the log.
这家人曾向船长正式投诉过，在航海日志里有记录。

soundly ['saʊndli] *adv.* 酣畅地

例 She was too soundly asleep to hear Stefano's return.
她睡得太熟，没有听见斯蒂芬诺回来。

inspect [ɪn'spekt] *v.* 检查；视察；检阅

例 Elaine went outside to inspect the playing field.
伊莱恩走到外面查看操场。

faithfully ['feɪθfəli] *adv.* 忠实地；如实地；诚心诚意地；深信着地

例 We took steps to ensure that rules should be faithfully carried.
我们采取了措施，以确保这些规章会不折不扣地得到贯彻。

语法知识点 Grammar points

① **He came to a small farm, which belonged to an old farmer and his wife.**

本句话为which引导的非限制性定语从句，非限制性定语从句中which不等同于that，非限制性定语从句起补充说明作用，是先行词的附加说明，去掉了也不会影响主句的意思，它与主句之间通常用逗号分开。

例 She was very patient towards the children, which her husband seldom was.
她对孩子们很耐心，她丈夫却很少这样。
He never has problems in his study, which was admired by his teacher.
他学习上从来没出过问题，他的老师很欣赏这点。

② **This answer quite puzzled the farmer and his wife. But he looked honest and reliable, so the couple liking the young man decided to hire him.**

decide to do 决定做……

例 When the weather began not to rain, I decided to go home.
当天没有下雨时，我决定回家。

decide相关的用法还有decide on 决定、选定，decide against 决定不，做出不利于……的判决。

例 Be sure that you decide on your colors well in advance.
确保实现选定你拍照要用的颜色。

The family have decided against buying the house in the country.
这家人已决定不买乡下的那座房子。

③ **They quickly began to check things out to see if all was secure.**

check out 检验；结账离开；通过考核；盖章

例 Well, what do you say we check out that swab then, huh?
那不如我们现在就开始检验吧，你说怎样？

if引导条件状语从句，表示"如果"

例 He will come if you invite him.
如果你邀请他，他会来的。

经典名句 Famous Classics

1. Life is made of ever so many partings welded together.
   人生是由许多部分焊接起来的整体。

2. Time, the devourer of everything.
   时间吞噬了一切。

3. It is not enough to be industrious, so are the ants. What are you industrious for?
   光勤劳是不够的，蚂蚁也是勤劳的。要看你为什么而勤劳。

4. Nothing is more precious than independence and freedom.
   没有什么比独立自由更可贵的了。

5. We are here to add what we can to life, not to get what we can from it.
   我们要尽可能为生活增加一些东西，而不是从中索取什么。

6. Life itself, without the assistance of colleges and universities, is becoming an advanced institution of learning.
   没有学院和大学的帮助，人生本身也正在变成一所高等学府。

7. Life is just a series of trying to make up your mind.
   生活只是由一系列下决心的努力所构成。

8. Early to bed and early to rise, makes a man healthy, wealthy, and wise.
   早睡早起使人健康、富裕又聪明。

9. Anything one man can imagine, other men can make real.
   但凡人能想象到的事物，必定有人能将它实现。

10. All human wisdom is summed up in two words: wait and hope.
    人类所有的智慧可以归结为两个词：等待和希望。

11. Do you love life? Then do not squander time; for that's the stuff life is made of.
    你热爱生命吗？那么，别浪费时间，因为生命是由时间组成的。

12. Fish and visitors smell three days.
    鱼放三天发臭，客住三天讨嫌。

10 A Little at a Time
循序渐进

I must have been about 14 then, and I dismissed the incident with the easy carelessness of youth. But the words Carl Walter spoke that day came back to me years later, and ever since have been of **inestimable** value to me.

Carl Walter was my piano teacher. During one of my lessons he asked how much practicing I was doing. I said three or four hours a day.

"Do you practice in long stretches, an hour at a time?"

"I try to."

"Well, don't." he exclaimed. "When you grow up, time won't come in long stretches. Practice in minutes, whenever you can find them, five or ten before school, after lunch, between chores. Spread the practice through the day, and piano-playing will become a part of your life."

When I was teaching at Columbia, I wanted to write, but **recitations**, theme-reading and committee meetings filled my days and evenings. For two years I got practically nothing down on paper, and my excuse was that Carl Walter had said.

当年我肯定有14岁了，但由于年少无知，我事后并没有做过多的思考。但是许多年后，我又想起了卡尔·沃尔特那天跟我说的话，那些话给我带来了不可估量的价值。

卡尔·沃尔特是我的钢琴老师。有一次上课时，他问我每天练琴多长时间，我回答说每天练三四个小时。

"你都用一整段的时间练琴吗？每次持续一个小时吗？"

"我尽量这样。"

"不，千万别这样！"他突然提高了音量说，"你长大以后，就不会有整段的时间去练琴了。利用一切可利用的时间，随时练琴。利用上学前、午饭后或是做家务时，空闲的五分钟或十分钟。把每天练琴的时间分散开来，这样弹钢琴就自然而然成为你生命的一部分了。"

当我在哥伦比亚教书时，希望写些文章，但是上课、批改作业以及开委员会议几乎占据了我的生活。在接下来的两年里，我事实上什么也没写，我为自己找的借口就是没时

A Little at a Time
循序渐进 **10**

During the next week I conducted an experiment. Whenever I had five minutes unoccupied, I sat down and wrote a hundred words or so. To my **astonishment**, I had a **sizable manuscript** ready for revision at the end of the week.

Later on I wrote novels by the same **piecemeal** method. Though my teaching schedule had become heavier than ever, every day there were idle moments which could be caught and put to use. I even took up piano-playing again, finding that the small **intervals** of the day provided sufficient time for both writing and piano practice.

There is an important trick in this time-using formula: You must get into your work quickly. If you have but five minutes for writing, you can't afford to waste four chewing your pencil. You must make your mental preparations beforehand, and concentrate on your task almost instantly when the time comes. Fortunately, rapid **concentration** is easier than most of us realize.

I **confess** I have never learned how to let go easily at the end of the five or ten minutes. But life can be counted on to supply interruptions. Carl Walter has had a **tremendous** influence on my life. To him I owe the discovery that even very short periods of time add up to all

之后，我回想起卡尔·沃尔特跟我说过的话。

在接下来的一周里，我做了个实验。只要有五分钟的空闲时间，我就坐下来写上一百来个字。出乎我的意料，到了周末，我已经有数量可观的一部分底稿可供修改了。

后来，我用了同样的方法，把空闲时间利用起来写小说。尽管我的教学任务比以前更加繁重，但是每天我总能抓住一些空余时间，并把它们利用起来，我甚至又能开始弹钢琴了，我发现把每天那些短短的空闲时间加起来，足够我写写东西、弹弹钢琴了。

在施行这种利用时间的方案时，还有个重要的诀窍需要注意：你必须很快投入进去。如果你只有五分钟的写作时间，你就不能花四分钟时间拿着铅笔构思。你必须事先有足够的精神准备，一有时间就立刻投入要做的事中。幸运的是，迅速集中精力比我们大部分人想象的要容易很多。

坦白地讲，至今我还没有学会在间歇的五分钟或十分钟结束时如何轻易将手中的事放下。但生活能够保证不断地给我们提供许多这样短暂的空余时间。卡尔·沃尔特对我的一

the useful hours I need, if I plunge in without delay.

生产生了巨大的影响。正是他让我发现，如果我做事能毫不拖沓地立即投入，即使是十分短暂的空闲时间，只要都利用起来，也会累积成为我所需要的几小时。

单词解析 Word Analysis

inestimable [ɪn'estɪməbl] *adj.* 极贵重的，（大得）无法估计的，不可估量的

例 Human life is of inestimable value.
人的生命无价。

recitation [ˌresɪ'teɪʃn] *n.* 背诵；朗诵；讲述

例 She continued her recitation of the week's events.
她接着逐一讲述这一周发生的事。

astonishment [ə'stɒnɪʃmənt] *n.* 惊讶，惊奇

例 I spotted a shooting star which, to my astonishment, was bright green in color.
我看见一颗流星，使我大为惊奇的是，它居然是鲜亮的绿色。

sizable ['saɪzəbl] *adj.* 相当大的，颇大的

例 For the most part they had converted their small prebends into sizable paunches.
他们中的大部分人已靠着小小的俸禄养成了大腹便便者。

manuscript ['mænjuskrɪpt] *n.* 手稿，原稿，底稿

例 He had seen a manuscript of the book.
他见过这本书的手稿。

piecemeal ['piːsmiːl] *adj.* 一块一块的；一件一件的；零碎的

例 A lack of narrative drive leaves the reader with piecemeal vignettes.
叙述缺乏吸引力，读者读到的只是一些支离破碎的片段。

A Little at a Time 循序渐进 10

interval [ˈɪntəvl] *n.* 间隔时间

例 The ferry service has restarted after an interval of 12 years.
时隔12年之后，轮渡服务又重新开通了。

concentration [ˌkɒnsnˈtreɪʃn] *n.* 专心，专注；集中，集结

例 We lacked concentration and it cost us the goal and the game.
我们注意力不够集中，结果丢了球，输了比赛。
The area has one of the world's greatest concentrations of wildlife.
这个地区是世界上野生动物最为密集的区域之一。

confess [kənˈfes] *v.* 承认，供认

例 I must confess I'm not a great enthusiast for long political programmes.
我必须承认自己对时间很长的政治节目不是很热衷。

tremendous [trəˈmendəs] *adj.* 极大的，巨大的

例 There's tremendous tension between the local population and the refugees.
当地居民与难民之间关系非常紧张。

语法知识点 Grammar points

① I must have been about 14 then, and I dismissed the incident with the easy carelessness of youth

must have done/been表示对过去事情的肯定推测，该结构只用于肯定句。

例 It must have rained last night, for the ground is wet.
昨晚一定下雨了，因为地面还是湿的。

类似的结构还有should+have+done，意思是"本来应该做某事，而实际没做"。

例 Tom, you are too lazy. The work should have been finished yesterday.
汤姆，你太懒惰了，这项工作本来应该昨天就做完的。

057

could+have+done是虚拟语气，表示对过去事情的假设，意思是本来能够做某事而没有做。

例 He could have passed the exam, but he was too careless.
本来他能够通过考试，但是他太粗心。

② **To my astonishment, I had a sizable manuscript ready for revision at the end of the week. Later on I wrote novels by the same piecemeal method.**

later on 以后，日后

例 Steps taken now to maximize your health will pay dividends later on.
现在采取措施增强体质会使你日后受益。

③ **Though my teaching schedule had become heavier than ever, every day there were idle moments which could be caught and put to use.**

put to use 使用；利用

例 To put to use or service.
投入使用或服务于。

Henry decided to put his dictionary to use.
亨利决定利用他的字典。

④ **You must make your mental preparations beforehand, and concentrate on your task almost instantly when the time comes.**

concentrate on 专心于，把思想集中于

例 Many firms are concentrating on increasing their markets overseas.
许多公司正在集中精力开拓它们的海外市场。

经典名句 Famous Classics

1. The time of life is short; to spend that shortness basely, it would be too long.
人生苦短，若虚度年华，则短暂的人生就太长了。

A Little at a Time
循序渐进

2. The golden age is before us, not behind us.
   黄金时代在我们面前而不在我们背后。

3. Ordinary people merely think how they shall spend their time; a man of talent tries to use it.
   普通人只想到如何度过时间，有才能的人设法利用时间。

4. We always have time enough, if we will but use it aright.
   只要我们能善用时间，就永远不愁时间不够用。

5. Weep no more, no sigh, nor groan. Sorrow calls no time that's gone.
   别哭泣，别叹息，别呻吟；悲伤唤不回流逝的时光。

6. To choose time is to save time.
   合理安排时间就是节约时间。

7. Never leave that until tomorrow, which you can do today.
   今天的事不要拖到明天。

8. In delay there lies no plenty, Then come kiss me, sweet and twenty, Youth's a stuff that will not endure.
   迁延蹉跎，来日无多，二十丽姝，请来吻我，衰草枯杨，青春易过。

读书笔记

11 If the Dream Is Big Enough
如果梦想足够远大

I used to watch her from my kitchen window, she seemed so small as she **muscled** her way through the crowd of boys on the playground. The school was across the street from our home and I would often watch the kids as they played during recess. A sea of children, and yet to me, she stood out from them all.

I remember the first day I saw her playing basketball. I watched in wonder as she ran circles around the other kids. She managed to shoot jump shots just over their heads and into the net. The boys always tried to stop her but no one could.

I began to notice her at other times, basketball in hand, playing alone. She would practice **dribbling** and shooting over and over again, sometimes until dark. One day I asked her why she practiced so much. She looked directly in my eyes and without a moment of **hesitation** she said, "I want to go to college. The only way I can go is if I get a scholarship. I like basketball. I decided that if I were good enough, I would get a scholarship. I am going to play college basketball. I want to be the best. My Daddy told me if the dream is

我以前常常从我家厨房的窗户看到她，她强行挤过操场上的一群男孩子，对这些男孩们来说，她显得那么矮小。学校在我家的街对面，我经常看到孩子们在下课时间打球。尽管有一大群的孩子，但我觉得她是最吸引我注意的一个。

我记得第一次看到她打篮球的情景。看见她绕着其他孩子旁边游走的时候，我感到十分惊奇。她设法跳起投篮，球恰好越过那些孩子的头顶飞入篮筐。那些男孩总是拼命地阻止她，但没有人可以做得到。

另外一些时候，她一个人练球，我开始注意观察她的举动。她一般是一遍遍地练习运球和投篮，有时直到天黑。有一天，我问她为什么这么刻苦地练习。她直视着我的眼睛，不假思索地说："我想上大学。只有获得奖学金我才能有钱去上大学。因为我喜欢打篮球，所以我决定了，只要我成为一个出色的球员，我就能获得奖学金。我将能够到大学去打篮球。我想成为最棒的球员。

If the Dream Is Big Enough
如果梦想足够远大

big enough, the facts don't count." Then she smiled and ran towards the court to recap the routine I had seen over and over again.

Well, I had to give it to her—she was determined. I watched her through those junior high years and into high school. Every week, she led her **varsity** team to victory.

One day in her senior year, I saw her sitting in the grass, head cradled in her arms. I walked across the street and sat down in the cool grass beside her. Quietly I asked what was wrong. "Oh, nothing," came to a soft reply, "I'm just too short." The coach told her that at "5.5" she would probably never get to play for a top ranked team—much less offered a **scholarship**—so she should stop dreaming about college.

She was **heartbroken** and I felt my own throat tighten as I sensed her disappointment. I asked her if she had talked to her dad about it yet. She lifted her head from her hands and told me that her father said those coaches were wrong. They just didn't understand the power of a dream. He told her that if she really wanted to play for a good college, if she truly wanted a scholarship, that nothing could stop her except one thing—her own **attitude**. He told her again, "if the dream is big enough, the

我父亲告诉我说，如果梦想远大，就一定可以克服艰难险阻。"说完她笑了笑，跑向篮球场，又开始我之前见过的一遍又一遍的练习。

嘿，我真服了她——她是个有决心的人。我看着她这些年从初中升到高中。每个星期，由她带领的学校篮球队都能够获胜。

在她读高中的某一天，我看见她坐在草地上，头埋在臂弯里。因此，我穿过街道，坐到她旁边的清凉的草地上，轻轻地问她发生了什么事。她轻声回答："哦，没什么，只是我太矮了。"原来篮球教练告诉她，以她五英尺五英寸的身材，几乎是没有机会到一流的球队去打球的，更不用说会获得奖学金了，所以她应该放弃想上大学的梦想。

她很伤心，由于感受到了她的失望，我也觉得自己的喉咙发紧。我问她是否与她的爸爸谈过这件事。她从臂弯里抬起头，告诉我，她父亲说那些教练讲得不对。他们根本不懂得梦想的力量。她父亲说，如果她真的有心去代表一个好的大学打篮球，如果她真的想获得奖学金，任何东西也不能阻止她，除非她自己没有这个心。他又一

facts don't count."

The next year, as she and her team went to the Northern California **Championship** game, she was seen by a college **recruiter**. She was indeed offered a scholarship, a full ride, to a Division I, **NCAA** women's basketball team. She was going to get the college education that she had dreamed of and worked toward for all those years.

次跟她说:"如果梦想远大,就一定可以克服艰难险阻。"

第二年,当她和她的球队去参加北加利福尼亚州冠军赛时,她被一位大学的招生人员看中了。那所大学真的为她提供了一份全额奖学金,并且她进入了美国全国大学体育协会其中一个女子甲组篮球队。她将接受到她梦想的并为之奋斗了多年的大学教育。

单词解析 Word Analysis

muscle ['mʌsl] v. 加强;使劲搬动;使劲挤出 n. 肌肉

例 They call rowing the perfect sport. It exercises every major muscle group.
他们称划船是最佳运动,它可以锻炼每一处主要肌肉群。

dribbling ['drɪblɪŋ] n. 运球,带球;dribbling是动词dribble的现在分词,现在分词做名词

例 The girls lined up behind the starting line, ready to dribble the ball to the cone atthe other end of the court, and back again.
女孩子们在起跑线后站成一排,准备将篮球运到场地另一边的锥形标志,再运回来。

hesitation [ˌhezɪ'teɪʃn] n. 犹豫

例 He promised there would be no more hesitations in pursuing reforms.
他答应在推进改革这件事上不再迟疑不决。

varsity ['vɑːsəti] a. 大学代表队的

例 She has been in the playoffs every year since she made the varsity.
自从加入校队后,她每年都能参加季后赛。

If the Dream Is Big Enough 如果梦想足够远大 11

scholarship [ˈskɒləʃɪp] *n.* 奖学金；学术，知识

例 He got a scholarship to the Pratt Institute of Art.
他获得了普拉特艺术学院的奖学金。

I want to take advantage of your lifetime of scholarship.
我希望能够用到您一生的学识。

heartbroken [ˈhɑːtbrəʊkən] *adj.* 悲伤的

例 Was your daddy heartbroken when they got a divorce?
他们离婚时你爸爸是不是很伤心？

attitude [ˈætɪtjuːd] *n.* （尤指从行为中表现出来的）态度，看法

例 Being unemployed produces negative attitudes to work.
失业会产生对工作的消极态度。

championship [ˈtʃæmpiənʃɪp] *n.* 锦标赛，冠军赛

例 He was in contention for a place in the European championship squad.
他有望在欧洲锦标赛代表队中获得一席之地。

This season I expect us to retain the championship and win the European Cup.
这个赛季我期待我们能够保住冠军头衔，赢得欧洲杯。

recruiter [rɪˈkruːtə(r)] *n.* 招聘人员，征兵人员

例 The tele recruiter is prompted by a variety of questions, depending on your answers.
针对你不同的回答，这位考官还会提出些不同的问题。

NCAA *abbr.* （美国）全国大学生体育协会

例 The NCAA basketball championship was won by North Carolina.
北卡罗来纳大学在美国大学篮球联赛中夺魁。

语法知识点 *Grammar points*

> ① I watched in wonder as she ran circles around the other kids. She managed to shoot jump shots just over their heads and into the net. The boys always tried to stop her but no one could.

in wonder 惊奇地，惊讶地

例 Sissy had suddenly turned her head, and looked, in wonder, in pity, in sorrow.
西丝忽然转过头来，表示着惊讶、怜悯和悲愁。

run circles around在本句话中翻译为其本意"兜来转去"，其还有引申意为"比（某人）做得更好，远远超过（某人）"。

例 In spelling Mary could run circles around Ann any day.
在拼写方面，玛丽任何时候都可以远远赛过安。

manage to do 设法做成某事

例 Lots of people do good work, but only a few manage to do great work more than a few minutes a day.
很多人在做重要的工作，但只有很少的人花很少的时间做那些更重要的工作。

> ② Every week, she led her varsity team to victory.

lead sb. to victory 带领某人走向胜利

例 Hence one can see that, without an understanding of the characteristics of China's revolutionary war, it is impossible to direct it and lead it to victory.
由此可知，不了解中国革命战争的特点，就不能指导中国革命战争，就不能引导中国革命战争走上胜利的途径。

> ③ She was going to get the college education that she had dreamed of and worked toward for all those years.

本句为定语从句，先行词为education，所以引导词为that，也可用which。that/which在代物时常常可以通用，但只宜于用which不用that的情况有：

If the Dream Is Big Enough 如果梦想足够远大 11

关系代词前有介词时。
- 例 This is the hotel in which you will stay.
  这是你即将入住的酒店。

如有两个定语从句,其中一句的关系代词是that,另一句宜用which。
- 例 Let me show you the novel that I borrowed from the library which was newly open to us.
  我来给你看一下我从新开放的图书馆借的小说。

只能用that不能用which的情况有很多,如:
先行词是形容词最高级或者它的前面有形容词最高级时。
- 例 This is the best that has been used against air pollution in cities.
  这是用于对抗城市空气污染最好的产品。
  English is the most difficult subject that you will learn during these years.
  英语将是这几年中最难的学科。

先行词是序数词,或它的前面有一个序数词时。
- 例 He is the last person that I want to see.
  他是我最不想见的人。

经典名句 Famous Classics

1. A well-written life is almost as rare as a well-spent one.
   写得很好的生活和过得很好的生活几乎一样少。

2. Absence of occupation is not rest, a mind quite vacant is a mind distress.
   无所事事不是休息,十分空虚的心灵是痛苦的。

3. All the blessings we enjoy are the fruits of labor, toil, and self-denial, and study.
   我们得到的一切幸福都是劳动、辛苦、自我克制和学习的成果。

4. Blessed is the man who expects nothing, for he shall not be disappointed.
   一无所求的人是幸福的,因为他永远也不会失望。

065

5. For in all adversity of fortune the worst sort of misery is to have been happy.
   在所有不幸中，最不幸的事是曾经幸福过。

6. Call no man happy till he dies, he is at best but fortunate.
   人不进棺材，谁也称不上幸福，而至多不过是幸运。

7. Happiness grows at our own firesides, and is not to be picked in strangers' garden.
   幸福生长在我们自己的火炉边，而不能从别人的花园中采得。

读书笔记

12 Two Roads
两条道路

It was New Year's Night. An aged man was standing at a window. He raised his **mournful** eyes towards the deep blue sky, where the stars were floating like white lilies on the surface of a clear calm lake. Then he **cast** them on the earth, where few more hopeless people than himself now moved towards their certain goal—the tomb. He had already passed sixty of the stages leading to it, and he had brought from his journey nothing but errors and **remorse**. Now his health was poor, his mind vacant, his heart sorrowful, and his old age short of comforts.

The days of his youth appeared like dreams before him, and he recalled the serious moment when his father placed him at the entrance of the two roads—one leading to a peaceful, sunny place, covered with flowers, fruits and **resounding** with soft, sweet songs; the other leading to a deep, dark cave, which was endless, where poison flowed instead of water and where **devils** and poisonous snakes **hissed** and crawled.

He looked towards the sky and cried painfully, "Oh, youth, return!

除夕之夜，一位老人伫立窗前。他满眼哀伤，仰望着深蓝色的天空，那儿，星星如清澈平静的湖面上的朵朵白莲在漂移着；后来，他将目光投向地面，几个比他更加绝望的人正在走向人生的终点——坟墓。在通往人生终点的道路上，他已走过了60多个驿站，除了过失和悔恨，他一无所获。现在，他健康欠佳，精神空虚，心情忧郁，缺少晚年应有的舒适和安逸。

青春的岁月如梦幻般浮现在他眼前，他回想起父亲将他放在人生岔路口上的关键时刻，当时，他面前有两条路：一条通向和平宁静、阳光灿烂的地方，那里到处是花果，到处回荡着柔和甜美的歌声；另一条则通向黑暗无底的深渊，那里流淌着毒液而不是清水，恶魔肆虐，毒蛇嘶嘶爬动。

他仰望天空，痛苦地哭喊："哦，青春，你回来吧！哦，爸爸，请把我重新放到人生的路口上吧，我会做出更好的选择。"然而他的父亲和他

067

Oh, my father, place me once more at the entrance to life, and I'll choose the better way!" But both his father and the days of his youth had passed away.

He was the lights flowing away in the darkness. These were the days of his wasted life; he saw a star fall from the sky and disappeared, and this was the symbol of himself. His remorse, which was like a sharp arrow, struck deeply into his heart. Then he remembered his friends in his childhood, who entered on life together with him. But they had made their way to success and were now honored and happy on this New Year's night.

The clock in the high church tower struck and the sound made him remember his parents' early love for him. They had taught him and prayed to God for his good. But he chose the wrong way. With shame and grief he dared no longer look towards that heaven where his father lived. His darkened eyes were full of tears, and with a despairing effort, he burst out a cry: "Come back, my early days! Come back!"

And his youth did return, for all this was only a dream which he had on New Year's Night. He was still young though his faults were real; he had not yet entered the deep, dark **cave**, and he was still free to walk on the road which leads to the peaceful and sunny land.

的青春年华皆离他远去。

他看见灯消逝在黑暗中，那便是他虚度的时光；他看见一颗星星从空中陨落、消失，那是他自身的象征。悔恨如同一支利箭，深深地刺进他的心。接着，他想起童年时代的朋友，他们曾与他一同踏上人生的旅程，现已获得成功，受到人们的尊敬，此刻正在幸福中欢度除夕。

教堂塔顶的钟声响了，使他回忆起父母早年对他的爱，他们曾给予他谆谆教诲，曾为他的幸福祈祷上帝。可他偏偏选择人生的歧途。羞愧和忧伤使他再也不敢正视他父亲所在的天堂。他双眼黯然无光，饱噙着泪水，在绝望中，他拼力高喊："回来吧，我那逝去的年华！回来吧！"

青春真的回来了，因为以上所发生的一切只是他在除夕所做的一场梦。他仍旧年轻，当然他真的犯有过失；但还未坠入深渊；他仍然可以自由地走上通向宁静和光明的道路。

在人生路口徘徊，不知该不该选择光明大道的年轻人啊，你们千万要记住：当你青春已逝，双足在黑暗的群山中举步维艰，跌跌撞撞之时，你才痛心疾首地呼唤："哦，回来吧，

Those who still **linger** on the entrance of life, hesitating to choose the bright road, remember that when years are passed and your feet **stumble** on the dark mountains, you will cry bitterly, but in vain: "Oh, youth, return! Oh, give me back my early days!"

青春！哦，把我的美好年华还给我！"这只是徒劳无益。

单词解析 Word Analysis

mournful ['mɔːrnfl] *adj.* 悲恸的；悲哀的；令人惋惜的
例 She was mournful for the whole of the day.
她悲恸终日。

cast [kæst] *v.* 掷；抛；投；铸造；指定演员；加起来；投射（目光）
例 The angler cast his line into the stream.
那个垂钓者把渔线掷进了小溪里。

remorse [rɪ'mɔːrs] *n.* 懊悔；悔恨
例 He was filled with remorse for not believing her.
他因为没有相信她而懊悔不已。

resound [rɪ'zaʊnd] *v.* （使）回响；鸣响；驰名
例 The whole building resounded the siren's warning.
整个大楼回响着警报声。

devil ['devl] *n.* 魔鬼；淘气鬼；坏人；家伙；棘手的事
例 I bet you were a little devil when you were younger.
我猜你年轻的时候一定是个小淘气鬼。

hiss [hɪs] *v.* 发出嘘声（表示不满）；发嘶嘶声
例 Even if you don't like one of the players, you should not boo and hiss at them.
即使是你不喜欢其中的一个球员，你不应该对他们发出嘘声。

cave [keɪv] *n.* 洞穴；山洞
- 例 This cave was used by smugglers in the eighteenth century.
  这个洞穴是十八世纪走私的人使用的。

linger ['lɪŋgər] *v.* 徘徊；逗留；消磨；漫步
- 例 She lingered after the concert, hoping to meet the star.
  音乐会后她徘徊不去，希望能遇见明星。

stumble ['stʌmbl] *v.* 绊倒；蹒跚；犯错误；无意中发现
- 例 Any man may stumble into crime when among criminals.
  同犯罪分子混在一起，任何人都可能失足犯罪。

语法知识点 *Grammar points*

① **He raised his mournful eyes towards the deep blue sky, where the stars were floating like white lilies on the surface of a clear calm lake. Then he cast them on the earth, where few more hopeless people than himself now moved towards their certain goal—the tomb.**

这两个句子中各有一个where引导的定语从句，先行词是the deep blue sky 和the earth。

on the surface of 表面上；在外表上
- 例 The wet glass left a mark on the surface of the table.
  湿杯子在桌面上留下一个痕迹。

move towards 走向
- 例 The government's announcement is seen as a move towards settling the strike.
  政府的通告已被视为迈向解决罢工问题的一步。

② **The days of his youth appeared like dreams before him, and he recalled the serious moment when his father placed him at the entrance of the two roads—one leading to a peaceful, sunny place, covered with flowers, fruits and resounding with soft, sweet songs; the other leading to a deep, dark cave, which was endless, where poison flowed instead of water and where devils and poisonous snakes hissed and crawled.**

Two Roads 两条道路 12

这个句子较长，让我们分开来看。破折号前面是主句，破折号后面的内容是对the two roads的解释说明。前面有一个when引导的定语从句，先行词是the serious moment。

at the entrance of 在……的入口处

> Could you just wait at the entrance of the hall?
> 您能在大厅前等着吗？

破折号后面用分号连接两个独立的部分。最后有一个which引导的非限制性定语从句，先行词是a deep, dark cave, which在从句中充当主语成分。还有两个where引导的定语从句。

lead to 导致，引起；通向；把……带到

> The government's present course will only lead to disaster.
> 政府的现行方针后患无穷。

covered with 被……覆盖

> The hut was made of poles covered with grass mats.
> 茅屋用木杆搭成，上面以草席覆盖。
> The wounded man was covered with blood.

instead of 代替；而不是……

> I gave him advice instead of money.
> 我给了他忠告，而不是钱。

③ And his youth did return, for all this was only a dream which he had on New Year's Night.

for all this 尽管如此

> For all this wealth, he was unhappy.
> 尽管他富有，但他并不幸福。

把介词短语提前，后面的句子用倒装结构。还有一个which引导的定语从句，修饰先行词a dream, which在从句中充当宾语。

经典名句 Famous Classics

1. The four stages of man are infancy, childhood, adolescence and obsolescence.
   人生的四个阶段是：婴儿，童年，少年，以及退化期。

071

2. I worked half my life to be an overnight success, and still it took me by surprise.
我梦想了一辈子，想一夜成名，结果还是吃了一惊。

3. The enemy of society is middle class and the enemy of life is middle age.
社会的敌人是中产阶级，人生的敌人是中年时期。

4. To be able to look life in the face: That's worth living in a garret for, isn't it?
能够面对面地注视着生命，就算是住在小破阁楼里也值得了，不是吗?

5. There is an ecstasy that marks the summit of life, and beyond which life cannot rise. And such is the paradox of living, this ecstasy comes when one is most alive, and it comes as a complete forgetfulness that one is alive.
人的一生中总有某一个令他狂喜的顶峰，在那之后，生活难以再有提升。矛盾的是，在那个瞬间，人们往往在最充分地活着，而也是那个瞬间，人们忘了自己活着。

6. Early to bed and early to rise, makes a man healthy, wealthy and wise.
早睡早起会使人健康、富有和聪明。

7. Sloth, like rust, consumes faster than labor wears.
懒惰像生锈一样，比操劳更能消耗身体。

8. Ninety-nine percent of the failures come from people who have the habit of making excuses.
百分之九十九的失败都是因为人们惯于找借口。

9. The habit of reading is the only enjoyment in which there is no alloy; it lasts when all other pleasures fade.
阅读习惯是唯一没有其他混合成分的享乐，当其他快乐消失的时候，它仍经久不衰。

13 The Answer Is Right There Above You
希望就在前方

If you put a **buzzard** in a pen six to eight feet square and entirely open at the top, the bird, in spite of its ability to fly, will be an absolute **prisoner**. The reason is that a buzzard always begins a flight from the ground with a run of ten to twelve feet. Without space to run, as is its habit, it will not even attempt to fly, but remain a prisoner for life in a small **jail** with no top.

The ordinary bat that flies around at night, who is a **remarkable nimble** creature in the air, cannot take off from a level place. If it is placed on the floor or flat ground, all it can do is to shuffle about helplessly and, no doubt, painfully, until it reaches some slight **elevation** from which it can throw itself into the air. Then, at once, it takes off like a flash.

A **bumblebee** if dropped into an open **tumbler** will be there until it dies, unless it is taken out. It never sees the means of escape at the top, but persists in trying to find some way out through the sides near the bottom. It will seek a way where none exists, until it completely destroys itself.

如果把一只秃鹫放在一个6~8平方英尺的无顶围栏里，这只大鸟尽管会飞，也绝对会成为这栏中之囚。原因是秃鹫从地面起飞前总要先助跑10~12英尺的距离。这是它的习惯，如果没有了足够的助跑空间，它甚至不会尝试去飞，只会终身困囿于一个无顶的小囚笼中。

晚上飞来飞去的普通的蝙蝠，本是一种在空中极其敏捷的动物，但却无法在平地上起飞。如果被放在地板或平坦的地面上，它就只会无助地挪动，毫无疑问这样很痛苦。除非它到了稍高的位置，有了落差，才可以立刻闪电般地起飞。

一只大黄蜂如果掉进了一个敞口平底玻璃杯里，除非有人把它拿出来，否则它就会一直待在里边直到死去。它永远不知道可以从杯口逃出，只坚持试图从杯底的四壁寻找出路。它会在根本不存在出口的地方寻找出路，直到彻底毁了自己。

在生活中，很多次我们

我的人生美文：那些随风飘逝的日子

Many times in our lives, we are dropped, crumpled, and ground into the dirt by the decisions we make and the **circumstances** that come our way. But no matter what happened or what will happen, we should never lose our value and hope, remember to look up and hope may be right there above us. Sometimes, in many ways, there are lots of people like the buzzard, the bat and the bumblebee. They are struggling about with all their problems and frustrations, not realizing that the answer is right there above them.

被自己制定的决策和身边的环境所抛弃、践踏，甚至碾入尘土。我们感到自己一无是处。但是不管发生了什么，或者将要发生什么，我们都永远不会失去自己的价值和希望，记住，抬起头希望就在眼前。有时候，其实在很多方面，很多人也像秃鹫、蝙蝠和大黄蜂一样，使尽浑身解数试图解决问题、克服挫折，却没有意识到解决之道就在正上方。

单词解析 Word Analysis

buzzard ['bʌzəd] *n.* 秃鹰类；贪婪卑鄙的小人

例 American vulture smaller than the turkey buzzard.
美洲秃鹫比红头兀鹰小。

prisoner ['prɪznə(r)] *n.* 囚犯，犯人；俘虏；刑事被告

例 One prisoner was still holding out on the roof of the jail.
一名犯人仍在监狱的房顶上顽抗。

He was held prisoner in Vietnam from 1966 to 1973.
他在1966年到1973年间被作为战俘关押在越南。

jail [dʒeɪl] *n.* 监狱；监牢；拘留所 *v.* 使入狱；监禁

例 Three prisoners escaped from a jail.
3名囚犯越狱了。

He was jailed for twenty years.
他被判了20年监禁。

The Answer Is Right There Above You
希望就在前方 13

remarkable [rɪ'mɑːkəbl] *a.* 卓越的；非凡的；值得注意的

例 It was a remarkable achievement.
那是一项非凡的成就。

nimble ['nɪmbl] *adj.* 敏捷的；聪明的；敏感的

例 Everything had been stitched by Molly's nimble fingers.
每一件东西都是莫莉灵巧的双手缝制出来的。
Elderly people are told that if they want to keep their minds nimble, they must use them.
老年人被告知，要想保持头脑灵敏，就必须要多动脑。

elevation [ˌelɪ'veɪʃn] *n.* 海拔；高地；提高；正面图；崇高

例 We're probably at an elevation of about 13,000 feet above sea level.
我们可能在大约海拔13,000英尺的高度。

bumblebee ['bʌmblbiː] *n.* 大黄蜂

例 In a word, physicists noted that flying, was impossible to bumblebee.
简单地说，大黄蜂这种生物，根本是不可能飞得起来的。

tumbler ['tʌmblə(r)] *n.* 平底玻璃杯

例 He took a tumbler from a cupboard.
他从碗橱里拿出一只平底玻璃杯。

circumstance ['sɜːkəmstəns] *n.* 环境，情况；事件；境遇

例 You should soon accommodate yourself to the new circumstance.
你应尽快适应新环境。
The strategy was too dangerous in the explosive circumstances of the times.
在当时那种一触即发的形势下，采取那样的策略太危险了。

语法知识点 *Grammar points*

① **If you put a buzzard in a pen six to eight feet square and entirely open at the top, the bird, in spite of its ability to fly, will be an absolute prisoner.**

in spite of 虽然，尽管

例 In spite of the extremity of her seclusion she was sane.
尽管完全与世隔绝，她依然心智健全。

② **The reason is that a buzzard always begins a flight from the ground with a run of ten to twelve feet.**

the reason is that... 原因是……

例 Part of the reason is that we are facing our problems in the wrong way.
这其中一部分原因是因为我们面对困难的方法有问题。

③ **The ordinary bat that flies around at night, who is a remarkable nimble creature in the air, cannot take off from a level place.**

该句的主干为 the ordinary bat..., cannot...，其中who引导的句子是定语从句，bat是先行词。

④ **It never sees the means of escape at the top, but persists in trying to find some way out through the sides near the bottom.**

它永远不知道可以从杯口逃出，只坚持试图从杯底的四壁寻找出路。
means of escape 逃脱的方法 means 方式，方法

例 The move is a means to fight crime.
采取这项举措是为了打击犯罪。

persist in doing 坚持；固执于

例 If you persist in misbehaving, you'll be punished.
如果你坚持胡作非为，就将受到惩罚。

⑤ **But no matter what happened or what will happen, we should never lose our value and hope, remember to look up and hope may be right there above us.**

The Answer Is Right There Above You
希望就在前方 13

no matter＋疑问词意为"无论……""不论……",用来引导让步状语从句。如: no matter who / whom（无论谁）, no matter what（无论什么）, no matter which（无论哪一个）, no matter how（无论怎样）等。

例 No matter what may happen, they've decided to leave this evening.
不管发生什么事,他们已决定今晚离开。

You are always welcome no matter where you are.
无论在何地,您总是会受到欢迎的。

经典名句 Famous Classics

1. It is not easy to find happiness in ourselves, and it is not possible to find it elsewhere.
要在自身找到幸福是不容易的,要在别的地方找到幸福则是不可能的。

2. Industry is fortune's right hand, and frugality is her left.
勤劳是财富的右手,节俭是她的左手。

3. Human felicity is produced not so much by great pieces of good fortune that seldom happen, as by little advantages that occur every day.
与其说人类的幸福来自偶尔发生的红运,不如说来自每天都有的小实惠。

4. Hope is itself a species of happiness which this world affords.
希望本身是一种幸福,也许是这个世界能提供的主要的幸福。

5. Happiness lies not in the mere possession of money; it lies in the joy of achievement, in the thrill of creative effort.
幸福不在于拥有金钱,而在于获得成就时的喜悦以及产生创造力的激情。

6. Happiness is not something you experience; it's something you remember.
幸福不是你经历的事,而是你记得的事。

7. No society can surely be flourishing and happy, of which the far greater part of the members are poor and miserable.
如果一个社会中的大部分成员贫穷而又悲惨,这个社会就谈不上繁荣幸福。

8. Nothing is more fatal to happiness than the remembrance of happiness.
没有什么比回忆幸福更令人痛苦的了。

9. Jobs and work do much more than most of us realize to provide happiness and contentment.
职业和工作在使人得到幸福与满足方面所起的作用比我们大多数意识到的要多得多。

10. Man is the artificer of his own happiness.
人是自己幸福的设计者。

14 Great Expectations
最高期望值

Pete Rose, the famous baseball player, whom I have never met, taught me something so valuable that changed my life. Pete was being interviewed in spring training the year he was about to break Ty Cobb's all time hits record. One reporter blurted out, "Pete, you only need 78 hits to break the record. How many **at-bats** do you think you'll need to get the 78 hits?" Without hesitation, Pete just stared at the reporter and very **matter-of-factly** said, "78." The reporter yelled back, "Ah, come on Pete, you don't expect to get 78 hits in 78 at-bats, do you?"

Mr. Rose calmly shared his **philosophy** with the **throngs** of reporters who were **anxiously** awaiting his reply to this seemingly **boastful** claim. "Every time I step up to the plate, I expect to get a hit! If I don't expect to get a hit, I have no right to step in the **batter's box** in the first place!" "If I go up hoping to get a hit," he continued, "then I probably don't have a prayer of getting a hit. It is positive expectation that has gotten me all of the hits in the first place."

我虽然没有机会和著名的棒球运动员皮特·罗斯见上一面，但是却从他那儿学到了意义重大且改变了我人生的东西。在一次春季训练期间皮特接受记者采访，那年他的击球纪录接近打破棒球老前辈泰·柯布的总击球纪录。当时一个记者脱口说道："皮特，你只差78个击球就能打破纪录，那么你认为你需要多少次击球机会就能得到78个击中球？"皮特直视着那个记者，马上以一种实事求是的语气回答："78次。"那个记者叫道："啊？拜托！皮特！你指望78次挥棒就一定击中78次球，不会吧？"

一大群记者迫不及待地想看看皮特·罗斯先生究竟如何解释自己刚才夸下的海口。他泰然自若地向记者们阐述他的观点："我每一次上垒都指望击中球！如果我不指望击中，我就不该第一个上击球位。"他接着说："如果我一上前就希望击中球，我可能就不用祈求神保佑我第二次击球了。就是这种积极的期望使我能够在这么多的

When I thought about Pete Rose's philosophy and how it applied to everyday life, I felt a little embarrassed. As a business person, I was hoping to make my sales **quotas**. As a father, I was hoping to be a good dad. As a married man, I was hoping to be a good husband. The truth was that I was an adequate **salesperson**, I was not so bad of a father, and I was an Okay husband. I immediately decided that being Okay was not enough!

I wanted to be a great salesperson, a great father and a great husband. I changed my attitude to one of **positive** expectation, and the results were amazing. I was fortunate enough to win a few sales trips, I won Coach of the Year in my son's baseball league, and I share a loving relationship with my wife, Karen, with whom I expect to be married to for the rest of my life! Thanks, Mr. Rose!

第一击就击中球。"

我琢磨了一下皮特·罗斯的人生观，这种人生观又何尝不适用于人们每天的生活呢？想到这儿，我感到有些惭愧。一直以来，作为一个生意人，我希望提高销售额；作为一个父亲，我希望自己是个好爸爸；作为一个已婚的人，我希望自己是好丈夫。实际上，我的工作干得勉勉强强，父亲当得马马虎虎，丈夫做得凑凑合合。想到这儿，我立即意识到仅仅做到"还凑合"是不够的。

我要成为一个成功的销售员，一个了不起的父亲和一个体贴的丈夫。于是我改变了自己的人生态度，我的期望变得更加积极了，其结果自然令人吃惊。我有幸赢得了几次销售旅行，还当选了儿子所在学校棒球队的年度最佳教练，我也和妻子卡伦和和睦睦恩爱有佳，期望我们必将相伴一生！谢谢你，罗斯先生！

单词解析 Word Analysis

at-bat n. （棒球）上场击

例 Charles was at bat only a short time before he struck out.
查尔斯击球不到一会就因三击不中而退场了。

Great Expectations 最高期望值 14

matter-of-factly *adv.* 实事求是地

例 The specialist told her about it matter-of-factly, like reading a shopping list.
专家平静地把这件事告诉了她，就好像在读一份购物清单。
"She thinks you're a spy," Scott said matter-of-factly.
"她认为你是间谍。"斯科特面不改色地说。

philosophy [fə'lɒsəfi] *n.* 哲学；哲理；人生观

例 They asked her some searching questions on moral philosophy and logic.
他们深入询问了她一些有关伦理学和逻辑学的问题。

anxiously ['æŋkʃəslɪ] *adv.* 焦急地，担忧地；急切的，渴望的

例 A friend of mine is a very anxious person.
我的一个朋友是个非常容易焦虑不安的人。
He is anxious that there should be no delay.
他非常希望不会出现延误。

throng [θrɒŋ] *n.* 人群；众多　*v.* 群集；蜂拥而至；挤满

例 A great throng packed out the theater and overflowed into the corridors.
一大群人坐满剧院并且还有人涌到了走廊上。
They throng the beaches between late June and early August.
6月底到8月初，他们群聚在海滩上。

boastful ['bəʊstfl] *adj.* 自夸的；自负的；喜夸耀的

例 I tried to emphasize my good points without sounding boastful.
我在强调自己的优点时尽量不让人觉得是在自我吹嘘。
I'm not being boastful.
我不是在吹牛。

batter's box 击球框

例 The batter's legal position shall be with both feet within the batter's box.
打击合法位置必须双脚都站在打击框框内。

081

quota ['kwəʊtə] *n.* 配额；定额；限额
例 The quota of four tickets per person had been reduced to two.
每人可购买的票的限额已经由四张降至两张。

salesperson ['seɪlzpɜːsn] *n.* 售货员
例 The job is for a salesperson five days a week after school.
这个工作是当销售员，时间是放学后，每周五天。

positive ['pɒzətɪv] *adj.* 积极的，肯定的；[数] 正的；[医] 阳性的
例 You have to do everything you can. You have to work your hardest. And if you do, if you stay positive, then you have a shot at a silver lining.
你必须全力以赴，最大限度地去努力。如果你这么做，并且保持乐观，你就会看见乌云背后的幸福线。
The athlete received a two-year suspension following a positive drug test.
该运动员因尿检结果呈阳性而被停赛两年。
It's really a simple numbers game with negative and positive numbers.
它其实就是正负数的简单数字游戏。

语法知识点 Grammar points

① **Pete was being interviewed in spring training the year he was about to break Ty Cobb's all time hits record.**

be about to 表示即将发生的动作，在时间上指最近的将来。
例 The new school year is about to begin.
新学年开学在即。

② **One reporter blurted out, "Pete, you only need 78 hits to break the record."**

blurt out 开始说话，脱口而出
例 The standard is skilled to add to blurt out.
熟练的标准就是要达到不假思索地脱口而出。

Great Expectations 最高期望值 14

break the record 打破纪录

例 He set out to break the record for the English Channel swim.
他立志要打破横渡英吉利海峡的纪录。

③ "Every time I step up to the plate, I expect to get a hit! If I don't expect to get a hit, I have no right to step in the batter's box in the first place!"

a hit 轰动一时；成功而风靡一时的人物

例 Each one needs to be a hit and that is our commitment.
每一个都必须成功，这是我们的承诺。

have no right to 没有权利做……

例 The police have no right to seek into the lives of ordinary citizens without just cause.
没有正当理由，警察无权过问普通公民的生活。

④ The truth was that I was an adequate salesperson, I was not so bad of a father, and I was an okay husband.

the truth is that 事实上，通常用在作文中，引出一个事实。

例 The truth is that Pete never liked his rich Uncle John.
真相是彼得从来都不喜欢他那个有钱的叔叔约翰。

经典名句 Famous Classics

1. Wisdom in the mind is better than money in the hand.
   脑中有知识，胜过手中有金钱。

2. By reading we enrich the mind; by conversation we polish it.
   读书可以使我们的思想充实，谈话使其更臻完美。

3. Wise men learn by other men's mistakes; fools by their own.
   聪明人从别人的错误中学得教训；笨人则自己付出代价。

4. The greater the power, the more dangerous the abuse.
   权力越大，滥用职权的危险就越大。

5. There's only one corner of the universe you can be sure of improving, and that's your own self.

083

这个宇宙中只有一个角落你肯定可以改进，那就是你自己。

6. Suffering is the most powerful teacher of life.
   苦难是人生最伟大的老师。

7. Heaven never seals off all the exits.
   天无绝人之路。

8. Jack of all trades and master of none.
   门门精通，样样稀松。

9. Behind the mountains there are people to be found.
   天外有天，山外有山。

10. By doing we learn.
    经一事，长一智。

11. A man is not old as long as he is seeking something; a man is not old until regrets take the place of dream.
    只要一个人还有追求，他就没有老；直到后悔取代了梦想，一个人才算老。

12. Do not aim for success if you want it; just do what you love and believe in, and it will come naturally.
    如果你想要成功，不要去追求成功；只管做你自己热爱的事情并相信它，成功自然到来。

读书笔记

15 Mirror, Mirror—What Do I See?
镜子，镜子，告诉我

A loving person lives in a loving world. A **hostile** person lives in a hostile world. Everyone you meet is your mirror.

Mirrors have a very particular function. They reflect the image in front of them. Just as a physical mirror serves as the vehicle to reflection, so do all of the people in our lives.

When we see something beautiful such as a flower garden, that garden serves as a **reflection**. In order to see the beauty in front of us, we must be able to see the beauty inside of ourselves. When we love someone, it's a reflection of loving ourselves. When we love someone, it's a reflection of loving ourselves. We have often heard things like "I love how I am when I'm with that person." That simply translates into "I'm able to love me when I love that other person." **Oftentimes**, when we meet someone new, we feel as though we "**click**". Sometimes it's as if we've known each other for a long time. That feeling can come from sharing similarities.

Just as the "mirror" or other person can be a positive reflection, it is more

充满爱意的人生活在充满爱意的世界里，充满敌意的人则生活在充满敌意的世界里。你所遇到的每一个人都是你的镜子。

镜子有一个非常独特的功能，那就是映射出在其前面的影像。就像真正的镜子具有反射功能一样，我们生活中的所有人也都能映射出他人的影子。

当我们看到美丽的事物时，例如一座花园，那这花园就起到了反射作用。为了发现我们面前美好的事物，我们必须能发现自己内在的美。我们爱某个人，也正是我们爱自己的表现。我们经常听到这样的话："当我和那个人在一起的时候，我爱那时的自己。"这句话也可以简单地说成："在我爱那个人的同时，我也能爱我自己。"有时，我们遇见一个陌生人，感觉仿佛是一见如故，就好像我们已经相识甚久。这种熟悉感可能来自于彼此身上的共同点。

就像"镜子"或他人能映射出我们积极的一面一样，我

likely that we'll notice it when it has a negative **connotation**. For example, it's easy to remember times when we have met someone we're not particularly crazy about. We may have some criticism in our mind about the person. This is especially true when we get to know someone with whom we would rather spend less time. Frequently, when we dislike qualities in other people, **ironically**, it's usually the mirror that's speaking to us. I began questioning myself further each time.

I encountered **so**meone that I didn't particularly like. Each time, I asked myself, "What is it about that person that I don't like?" and then "Is there something similar in me?" in every instance, I could see a piece of that quality in me, and sometimes I had to really get very **introspective**. So what did that mean?

It means that just as I can get annoyed or disturbed when I notice that aspect in someone else, I better **reexamine** my qualities and consider making some changes. Even if I'm not willing to make a **drastic** change, at least I consider how I might **modify** some of the things that I'm doing.

At times we meet someone new and feel distant, disconnected, or disgusted.

们更有可能注意到映射出自己消极方面的"镜子"。例如，我们很容易就能记住我们碰到自己不太喜欢的人的时刻。我们可能在心里对那个人有些反感。当我们认识自己不喜欢与之相处的人时，这种情况就更为明显。具有讽刺意味的是，通常当我们讨厌别人身上的某些特质时，那就说明你其实讨厌自己身上相类似的特质。

每次，当我遇到不太喜欢的人时，我就开始进一步质问自己。我会扪心自问："我不喜欢那个人的哪些方面？"然后还会问："我是不是有和他相似的地方？"每次，我都能在自己身上看到一些令我厌恶的特质。我有时不得不深刻地反省自己。那这意味着什么呢？

这意味着，就像我会对其他人身上令我厌恶的特质感到恼怒或不安一样，我应该更好地重新审视自己的特质，并考虑做一些改变。即使我不想做大的改变，至少我会考虑该如何修正自己正在做的一些事情。

我们时常会遇到陌生人，并感到疏远或厌恶。尽管我们不想去相信，不容易也不想去深究，但是弄清楚别人的哪些特质在自己身上有所体现是非

Mirror, Mirror—What Do I See?
镜子，镜子，告诉我

Although we don't want to believe it, and it's not easy or **desirable** to look further, it can be a great learning lesson to figure out what part of the person is being reflected in you. It's simply just another way to create more self-awareness.

常有意义的一课，这也正是增强自我意识的另一个途径。

单词解析 Word Analysis

hostile ['hɒstaɪl] *a.* 敌对的，怀敌意的

例 The West has gradually relaxed its hostile attitude to this influential state.
西方对这个颇具影响力的国家的敌视态度已逐渐缓和。
Drinking may make a person feel relaxed and happy, or it may make her hostile, violent, or depressed.
喝酒可能让人感到放松和愉快，也可能让人变得不友善、暴力或阴郁。

reflection [rɪˈflekʃn] *n.* 反映，沉思，映像

例 After days of reflection she decided to write back.
想了几天之后她决定回信。
Inhibition in adulthood seems to be very clearly a reflection of a person's experiences as a child.
一个人成年期的情感压抑似乎很明显是其童年时期经历的反映。

oftentimes [ˈɒfntaɪmz] *adv.* 时常地

例 They can finish the training oftentimes without any injuries.
他们常常能够毫发无损地完成训练。

click [klɪk] *v.* 使发咔嗒声；点击

例 The applause rose to a crescendo and cameras clicked.
掌声越来越响，照相机的咔嗒声不绝于耳。
I clicked on a link and recent reviews of the production came up.
我点击了一个链接，有关该剧的最新评论弹了出来。

connotation [ˌkɒnəˈteɪʃn] *n.* 含义

例 A possible connotation of "home" is a place of warmth, comfort and affection.
"家"的可能含义是一个温暖、舒适和爱的地方。

ironically [aɪˈrɒnɪklɪ] *adv.* 说反话地，讽刺地

例 Ironically, the murderer was killed with his own gun.
饶有讽刺意味的是，杀人者被自己的枪所击毙。

introspective [ˌɪntrəˈspektɪv] *adj.* 内省的，反省的

例 Satire is a lonely and introspective occupation.
讽刺是一项孤独而又内省的工作。

reexamine [ˌriːɪɡˈzæmɪn] *v.* 复试，再调查

例 We may reexamine our goals or our methods for attaining our goals.
我们可能会重新审视我们的目标或我们实现目标的方法。

drastic [ˈdræstɪk] *adj.* 激烈的，猛烈的

例 Drastic measures are needed to clean up the profession.
行业清理整顿需要严厉的措施。

modify [ˈmɒdɪfaɪ] *v.* 修改，修饰

例 The club members did agree to modify their recruitment policy.
俱乐部成员的确同意修改吸纳新成员的政策。

desirable [dɪˈzaɪərəbl] *adj.* 令人满意的，值得要的

例 Prolonged negotiation was not desirable.
拖长了的谈判并不是大家所想要的。

语法知识点 Grammar points

① We may have some criticism in our mind about the person. This is especially true when we get to know someone with whom we would rather spend less time.

in one's mind 在……心里

Mirror, Mirror—What Do I See?
镜子，镜子，告诉我　15

> Whatever was in Warhol's mind that one would have to do amount of digging.
> 无论沃霍尔脑子想的是什么，你都得为此挖掘一下。

would rather 宁愿……（而）不愿……，与其……倒不如……
常用句型 would rather do sth. than do sth.

> To enjoy the scenery, Irene would rather spend long hours on the train than travel by air.
> 为了享受旅途风景，艾琳宁愿坐长途火车也不愿乘坐飞机。

② **I began questioning myself further each time. I encountered someone that I didn't particularly like.**

each time 每一次

> Each time I see him, he looks miserable.
> 每次我看到他，他都是一副愁眉苦脸的样子。

③ **Even if I'm not willing to make a drastic change, at least I consider how I might modify some of the things that I'm doing.**

be willing to do sth. 乐意做某事

> A great man is always willing to be little.
> 伟大的人物总是愿意当小人物的。

even if 即使，纵然，哪怕

> Friendship means understanding, not agreement. It means forgiveness, not forgetting. It means the memories last, even if contact is lost.
> 友情是理解，不是妥协；是原谅，不是遗忘。即使不联系，感情依然在。

④ **It can be a great learning lesson to figure out what part of the person is being reflected in you.**

该句中，what part of the person is being reflected in you 是作为 figure out 的宾语，为宾语从句。

figure out 理解，想出，计算出

> No one can figure out how the fire started.
> 没有人弄得清这场火灾是怎么引发的。

经典名句 Famous Classics

1. If you were a tear in my eye I would never want to cry because I would be scared to lose you.
   如果你是我眼中的一滴泪，我永远都不会哭，因为我怕那样会失去你。

2. The best time to make friends is before you need them.
   不要等到需要别人帮助的时候，才想着去和人家攀交情。

3. A pessimist sees the difficulty in every opportunity; an optimist sees the opportunity in every difficulty.
   悲观者从机遇中看到困难，乐观者从困难中看到机遇。

4. I hope you spend your time with someone you love, even it's just you.
   我希望你能跟自己喜欢的人在一起，即使你喜欢的人只有你自己。

5. The greatest mistake you can make in life is to be continually fearing you will make a mistake.
   人生中最大的错误是不断纠结于自己会不会犯错。

6. All our dreams can come true, if we have the courage to pursue them.
   我们的所有梦想都能实现，只要我们有勇气去追求。

7. In order to do really great things, you need to make really great mistakes.
   不犯巨大的错误就不能取得伟大的成就。

8. The future is something which everyone reaches at the rate of sixty minutes an hour, whatever he does, whoever he is.
   未来是这样一件东西，每个人都以每小时六十分钟的速度朝它走去，不管他做什么，也不管他是谁。

16 How to Be True to Yourself
如何做个表里如一的人

My grandparents believed you were either honest or you weren't. There was no in between. They had a simple **motto** hanging on their living-room wall: "Life is like a field of newly fallen snow; where I choose to walk every step will show." They didn't have to talk about it—they demonstrated the motto by the way they lived.

They understood **instinctively** that **integrity** means having a personal standard of morality and ethics that does not sell out to selfishness and that is not relative to the situation at hand. Integrity is an inner standard for judging your behavior. Unfortunately, integrity is in short supply today—and getting scarcer. But it is the real **bottom** line in every area of society. And it is something we must demand of ourselves.

A good test for this value is to look at what I call the Integrity Trial, which consists of three key principles:

Stand firmly for your convictions in the face of personal pressure. There's a story told about a surgical nurse's first day on the medical team at a well-known hospital. She was responsible

我的爷爷和奶奶认为,你要么是诚实的,要么不是,不可能介于两者之间。在他们起居室的墙上挂着一幅简单易懂的座右铭:"生活好像一片刚刚落满白雪的土地,我走到哪里,我的每一个脚印就会出现在哪里。"他们无须就此加以评说——他们是以身体力行的方式来证实这幅座右铭的。

他们本能的理解是,诚实意味着具备一定的伦理道德标准,既不见风使舵,也不随着眼下的形势而转移。诚实是判断你行为的内在标准。遗憾的是,如今,诚实处在短缺状态——甚至越来越稀罕。然而,它却是社会各个领域真正的思想底线,而且是我们必须要求自己严格做到的。

检验这种价值标准的一个有效方法是,参看我所指的诚实考验,其中包括三条主要原则:

面对个人压力,坚守自己的信念。有这么个故事,说的是一个外科护士在一所著名医院的一个小组里第一天工作

for ensuring that all instruments and materials were accounted for during an **abdominal** operation. The nurse said to the surgeon. "You've only removed 11 sponges, and we used 12. We need to find the last one."

"I removed them all," The doctor declared, "We'll close now."

"You can't do that, sir," objected the rookie nurse, "Think of the patient."

Smiling, the surgeon lifted his foot and showed the nurse the 12th **sponge**. "You'll do just fine in this or any other hospital," He told her.

When you know you're right, you can't back down. Always give others credit that is rightfully theirs. Don't be afraid of those who might have a better idea or who might even be smarter than you are.

Be honest and open about who you really are. People who lack genuine core values rely on external factors—their looks or status—in order to feel good about themselves. **Inevitably** they will do everything they can to preserve this appearance, but they will do very little, to develop their inner value and personal growth.

So be yourself. Don't engage in a personal cover-up of areas that are unpleasing in your life. When it's tough, do it tough. In other words, face reality and be adult in your responses to life's

的事。在一个腹腔手术中，她负责查点所有的器械和物品数量。这个护士对医生说："您只取出了11块纱布，可我们用了12块。我们得找到最后的那一块。"

"我都取出来了，"医生肯定地说，"现在我们要缝合了。"

"您不能这么做，先生，"这个护士反对道，"要替病人想想。"

医生笑着抬起脚，护士看到了那第12块纱布。他对护士说："无论在这家医院或是其他任何一个医院里，你都会干得很出色。"

当你知道你没错时，你就不能退缩。一定承认属于他人的荣誉。不要惧怕那些可能想法比你更高明，或是那些比你还聪明的人。

真诚、坦率地展示真实的你。那些缺乏真正的基本价值观念的人，为了使自己感觉良好而依靠外在因素——相貌或社会地位。他们势必尽一切可能来保全这种表面形象，却很少会去培养自己内在的价值和注重个人的成长。

因此，要展示你的真面目。不要设法掩盖你生活中令人不快的方方面面。艰难时刻要顽强。换言之，要正视现

How to Be True to Yourself
如何做个表里如一的人

challenges.

Self-respect and a clear **conscience** are powerful components of integrity and are the basis for enriching your relationships with others.

Integrity means you do what you do because it's right and not just fashionable or politically correct. A life of principle, of not giving in to the **seductive** sirens of easy morality, will always win the day. It will take you forward into the 21st century without having to check your tacks in a rear-view mirror. My grandparents taught me that.

实。面对生活的挑战，要老成持重，应付有方。

自尊和问心无愧是构成诚实的强有力的成分，是丰富你与他人关系的基础。

诚实意味着去做你认为对的事，而不仅仅是为了赶时髦或在政治正确。坚持原则，不屈从于持享乐人生观的女妖的诱惑，这样的人生观将战无不胜。它将使你问心无愧地走向21世纪。这是祖父母教导我的。

单词解析 *Word Analysis*

motto [ˈmɒtəʊ] *n.* 座右铭，箴言

例 Our motto is "Plan for the worst and hope for the best".
我们的格言是"做最坏的打算，抱最大的希望"。

instinctively [ɪnˈstɪŋktɪvlɪ] *adv.* 本能地

例 Jane instinctively knew all was not well with her 10-month old son.
简凭直觉知道她10个月大的儿子情况不对劲。

integrity [ɪnˈtegrəti] *n.* 真诚，诚实；完整，完全，完善

例 I have always regarded him as a man of integrity.
我一直认为他正直诚实。

Separatist movements are a threat to the integrity of the nation.
分离主义运动对国家统一是个威胁。

bottom [ˈbɒtəm] *n.* 底部；末端；尽头 *adj.* 最下方的，底部的

例 Answers can be found at the bottom of page 8.
在第8页末尾可以找到答案。

There's an extra duvet in the bottom drawer of the cupboard.
橱柜最底层的抽屉里还有一床羽绒被。

abdominal [æb'dɒmɪnl] *adj.* 腹部的
例 These stomach exercises will tighten abdominal muscles.
这些腹部练习会增强腹肌。

sponge [spʌndʒ] *n.* 纱布；绷带 *v.* 用湿海绵擦拭
例 Fill a bowl with water and gently sponge your face and body.
在盆里放上水，轻轻地用蘸湿的海绵擦拭你的面部及身体。
Cover the base with a single layer of sponge fingers.
底部垫上一层海绵条。

inevitably [ɪn'evɪtəbli] *adv.* 不可避免地，自然而然地；必然地，无疑地
例 Inevitably those who suffer the most are the mothers and children.
妇女和儿童必然是最遭罪的。

conscience ['kɒnʃəns] *n.* 良心，道德
例 What if he got a guilty conscience and brought it back?
要是他觉得内疚，把东西拿回来了怎么办？

seductive [sɪ'dʌktɪv] *adj.* 诱惑的，引诱的；有魅力的，性感的
例 It's a seductive argument.
这是一个非常吸引人的论点。

语法知识点 Grammar points

① **They understood instinctively that integrity means having a personal standard of morality and ethics that does not sell out to expediency and that is not relative to the situation at hand.**

本句的骨干结构为：... that... that... and that... 第一个that是动词understood的宾语从句，后两个that引导的是并列的定语从句，修饰先行词morality and ethics。

How to Be True to Yourself 如何做个表里如一的人 16

sell out 背叛；售完，售罄

例 Football games often sell out well in advance.
足球比赛经常在开赛前很久票就已经售光了。

② **Stand firmly for your convictions in the face of personal pressure.**

in the face of 面对

例 The policemen bore up to their duty in the face of the terrorists.
面对恐怖分子，警察始终忠于职守。

face 的相关短语 face to face 面对面 make faces 扮鬼脸

③ **Be honest and open about who you really are. People who lack genuine core values rely on external factors—their looks or status—in order to feel good about themselves.**

rely on 依靠，依赖，指望

例 Don't always rely on others to understand and sympathize.
不要老是指望别人的理解和同情。

external factors 外部因素，相对于 internal factors 内部因素

例 Language can change due to either internal or external factors.
语言的变迁有内因也有外因。

④ **A life of principle, of not succumbing to the seductive sirens of easy morality, will always win the day.**

seductive 诱惑的，引人注意的，有魅力的

例 Her figure was slighter and therefore more seductive than Natalie.
她的身段比较苗条，因此比娜塔丽更加诱人。

siren 塞壬（古希腊传说中半人半鸟的女海妖，惯以美妙的歌声引诱水手，使他们的船只触礁或驶入危险水域。）

win the day 打胜仗

经典名句 Famous Classics

1. The most wasted day of all is that during which we have not laughed.

095

最浪费的日子是没有笑声的日子。

2. If you wish to succeed, you should use persistence as your good friend, experience as your reference, prudence as your brother and hope as your sentry.
如果你希望成功，当以恒心为良友、以经验为参谋、以谨慎为兄弟、以希望为哨兵。

3. Life was like a box of chocolates, you never know what you're gonna get.
生活就像是满盒子各式各样的巧克力糖，你永远无法预计下一秒哪一颗会是你的。

4. You are where you are and what you are because of yourself. Everything you are today, or ever will be in the future, is up to you. Your life today is the sum total result of your choices, decisions and actions up to this point. You can create your own future by changing your behaviors. You can make new choices and decisions that are more consistent with the person you want to be and the things you want to accomplish with your life.
你现今的处境和状况，全都是自己一手打造的；而你的未来人生，也将由你自己一手造就。你过往的每一次选择、每一个决定、每一项行为，造成了今日的你。通过改变行为方式，你可以创造新的未来。你可以重新选择、重新决定，与你周遭的人更融洽协调，以达成期望的目标，开创成功人生。

读书笔记

17 If I Were a Boy Again
假如回到童年

"There are only two creatures," says a proverb; "who can **surmount** the pyramids—the eagle and the snail." If we want light, we must conquer darkness. **Perseverance** can sometimes equal genius in its results. If I were a boy again, I would practice perseverance more often, and never give up a thing because it was hard or **inconvenient**.

If I were a boy again, I would school myself into a habit of attention. I would let nothing come between me and the subject in hand. I would remember that a good skater never tries to skate in two directions at once. The habit of attention becomes part of our life, if we begin early enough. I often hear grown-up people say, "I could not fix my attention on the **sermon** or book, although I wished to do so," and the reason is, the habit was not formed in youth.

If I were to live my life over again, I would pay more attention to the **cultivation** of the memory. I would strengthen that faculty by every possible means and on every possible occasion. It takes a little hard work at first to remember things accurately; but

谚语说："能登上金字塔的生物只有两种——雄鹰与蜗牛。"如果我们需要光明，我们就得征服黑暗。在产生的结果方面，毅力往往可以与天才相媲美。假如我再回到童年，我会更多地培养自己的毅力，决不因为事情艰难或麻烦而放弃不干。

假如我再回到童年，我会培养自己专心致志的习惯；一旦手头有事，决不让任何东西使我分心。我会牢记：一位优秀的溜冰手从不试图同时滑向两个不同的方向。如果及早养成专心致志的习惯，它就会成为我们生命的一部分。我常常听到成年人说："尽管我希望集中注意力听讲课或读书，但往往做不到。"其原因就在于年轻时没有养成这种习惯。

假如我能重新活过，我会更加注意培养自己的记忆力。我要采取一切可能的办法，在一切可能的场合，增强记忆力。要精确地记住一切事物，起初的确要做出一番小小的努力；但用不了多久，记忆力本

memory soon helps itself, and gives very little trouble. It only needs early cultivation to become a power.

If I were a boy again, I would cultivate courage. "Nothing is so mild and gentle as courage, nothing so cruel and **pitiless** as **cowardice**," says a wise author. We too often borrow trouble, and anticipate that may never appear. The fear of ill exceeds the ill we fear. Dangers will arise in any career, but presence of mind will often conquer the worst of them. Be prepared for any fate, and there is no harm to be feared.

If I were a boy again, I would look on the cheerful side. Life is very much like a mirror: If you smile upon it, it smiles back upon you; but if you frown and look **doubtful** on it, you will get a similar look in return. Inner sunshine warms not only the heart of the owner, but of all that come in contact with it.

Who shuts love out, in turn shall be shut from love.

If I were a boy again, I would school myself to say "No" often. I might write pages on the importance of learning very early in life to gain that point where a young boy can stand erect and decline doing an unworthy act because it is **unworthy**.

If I were a boy again, I would

身就会起作用，使记忆成为轻而易举的事。只需及早培养，记忆自会成为一种才能。

假如我又回到了童年，我就要培养勇气。"世上没有东西比勇气更温文尔雅，也没有东西比怯懦更残酷无情。"一位明智的作家曾说过我们常常过多地自寻烦恼，杞人忧天。怕祸害比祸害本身更可怕，凡事都有危险，但镇定沉着往往能克服最严重的危险。对一切祸福做好准备，那么就没有什么灾难可以害怕的了。

假如我能再回到童年，我会凡事都看光明的一面。生活就像一面镜子：你朝它微笑，它也会朝你微笑。但如果你朝它皱眉头，它也会朝你皱眉头。内心的阳光不仅温暖了自己的心，同时也温暖了所有跟他接触的人的心。

谁将爱拒之门外，谁就会被爱拒之门外。

假如我再回到童年，我就要养成经常说"不"的习惯。我可以写上好几页，谈谈早期培养这一点的重要性，一个少年要能挺得起腰杆，拒绝做不值得做的事——就因为它不值得做。

假如我再回到童年，我

demand of myself more **courtesy** towards my companions and friends, and indeed towards strangers as well. The smallest courtesies along the rough roads of life are like the little birds that sing to us all winter long, and make that season of ice and snow more **endurable**. Finally, instead of trying hard to be happy, as if that were the sole purpose of life, I would, if I were a boy again, try still harder to make others happy.

会要求自己对待同伴和朋友更礼貌，而且对陌生人也同样如此。在坎坷的人生道路上，最细小的礼貌犹如在漫长的冬季为我们唱歌的小鸟，使得冰天雪地的严冬变得较易忍受。最后，假如我再回到童年，我不会竭力为自己谋幸福——仿佛那是人生的唯一目标；与之相反，我会更加努力让他人幸福。

单词解析 Word Analysis

surmount [sə'maʊnt] v. 战胜；处于……上面；置于……顶端

例 I realized I had to surmount the language barrier.
我意识到我不得不克服语言障碍。

The island is surmounted by a huge black castle.
岛的最高处耸立着一座巨大的黑色城堡。

perseverance [ˌpɜːsɪ'vɪərəns] n. 坚持不懈；不屈不挠

例 They showed great perseverance in the face of difficulty.
他们面对困难表现了坚强的毅力。

inconvenient [ˌɪnkən'viːniənt] adj. 不方便的；造成麻烦的

例 It's very inconvenient to have to wait so long.
等这么久很麻烦。

sermon ['sɜːmən] n. 布道，讲道，说教

例 The minister preaches a sermon now and then.
牧师不时地讲道。

Don't preach me a sermon, please.
请不要对我讲大道理。

cultivation [ˌkʌltɪ'veɪʃn] *n.* 培养
例 Cultivating a positive mental attitude towards yourself can reap tremendous benefits.
培养一种自信的积极心态会让人受益匪浅。

pitiless ['pɪtiləs] *adj.* 没有怜悯心的，无情的
例 He saw the pitiless eyes of his enemy.
他看到了敌人冷酷的眼神。

cowardice ['kaʊədɪs] *n.* 懦弱，胆怯
例 If he funks it, he will confirm the impression of cowardice given by his recent letter.
如果他对此畏缩，那就会证实他在最近一封信里表现出来的怯懦。

doubtful ['daʊtfl] *adj.* 怀疑的，拿不准的；难以预料的，未定局的
例 I was still very doubtful about the chances for success.
我对能否成功仍然深表怀疑。
Whether the authorities will allow inspection is highly doubtful.
当局是否允许检查还是个大问号。

unworthy [ʌn'wɜːði] *adj.* 不值得的，配不上的；与（某人）身份不相符的
例 You may feel unworthy of the attention and help people offer you.
你可能会觉得自己不值得别人关心和帮助。
His accusations are unworthy of a prime minister.
他的指责与其首相身份不相称。

courtesy ['kɜːtəsi] *n.* 谦恭有礼
例 He is a gentleman who behaves with the utmost courtesy towards ladies.
他是一位对女士极有风度的绅士。

endurable [ɪn'djʊərəbl] *adj.* 能持久的；耐用的；忍得住；恒久的
例 With ABS cover, strong and endurable, widely use for packing.
以ABS为外壳，具有坚固耐用的特点。

If I Were a Boy Again 假如回到童年 17

语法知识点 *Grammar points*

① **If I were a boy again, I would practice perseverance more often, and never give up a thing because it was inconvenient.**

此句子结构是If I were... , I would+动词原形+because... 含有与现在事实相反的虚拟语气。

例 If I were a bird, I would be able to fly in the air.
如果我是一只小鸟，我就能在空中飞行。

give up 放弃

例 Unless everyone can give up a little freedom of his own, otherwise no one can get along well with others.
除非人人都放弃自己的一点自由，否则谁也无法和别人愉快地相处。

② **Dangers will arise in any career, but presence of mind will often conquer the worst of them.**

presence of mind 沉着镇定

例 Because he had the presence of mind, the children were saved.
由于他沉着冷静，孩子们得救了。

③ **I might write pages on the importance of learning very early in life to gain that point where a young boy can stand erect and decline doing an unworthy act because it is unworthy.**

stand erect 矗立；屹立

例 Whenever he speaks with a lady, he would stand erect, cap in hand.
每当他与女士交谈时，他总是恭恭敬敬地站着。

decline 婉拒，谢绝；decline doing 谢绝做。decline最常用的意思"下降；减少；衰退；衰落"。

例 The number of staff has declined from 217,000 to 114,000.
员工人数从21.7万减少到了11.4万。

Hourly output by workers declined 1.3% in the first quarter.
第一季度工人每小时的产量下降了1.3%。

经典名句 Famous Classics

1. Opportunities are not offered. They must be wrested and worked for. And this calls for perseverance and courage.
   机会不会从天而降，必须怀揣坚持与勇气去努力争取。

2. Don't be disappointed on the journey of life, there are friends wherever you go. Seize your chance and value your opportunities, may our friendship be everlasting.
   人生路上何需惆怅，天涯海角总有知音。把握机会珍惜缘分，祝愿我们友谊长存。

3. Try not to become a man of success but rather try to become a man of value.
   不要为成为一个成功者而努力，而要为做一个有价值的人而努力。

4. One's real value first rests in to what degree and what sense he liberates from himself.
   一个人的真正价值首先取决于他在什么程度上和在什么意义上从自我解放出来。

5. We should fill ourselves with confidence as we fill ourselves every day with food.
   我们要以信心充实自己，就像我们每天以食物充实自己一样。

6. Sound heath is the greatest of gifts, contentedness, the greatest of riches, trust, the greatest of qualities.
   健康是最好的天赋，知足是最大的财富，信任是最佳的品德。

7. Experience is the name everyone gives to their mistakes.
   人们把自己经历过的失败叫作经验。

8. A great man shows his greatness by the way he treats little men.
   大人物通过善待小人物显示自己的伟大。

18 If I Rest I Rust
如果我休息，我就会生锈

The significant **inscription** found on an old key— "If I rest, I rust" —would be an excellent motto for those who are **afflicted** with the slightest bit of **idleness**. Even the most **industrious** person might adopt it with advantage to serve as a reminder that, if one allows his faculties to rest, like the iron in the unused key, they will soon show signs of rust and, ultimately, cannot do the work required of them.

Those who would attain the heights reached and kept by great men must keep their faculties polished by constant use, so that they may unlock the doors of knowledge, the gate that guard the entrances to the professions, to science, art, literature, agriculture—every department of human endeavor.

Industry keeps bright the key that opens the **treasury** of achievement. If Hugh Miller, after toiling all day in a quarry, had devoted his evenings to rest and **recreation**, he would never have become a famous geologist. The celebrated mathematician, Edmund Stone, would never have published a mathematical dictionary, never

在一把旧钥匙上发现了一则意义深远的铭文——如果我休息，我就会生锈。对于那些懒散而烦恼的人来说，这将是至理名言。甚至最为勤勉的人也以此作为警示：如果一个人有才能而不用，就像废弃钥匙上的铁一样，这些才能就会很快生锈，并最终无法完成安排给自己的工作。

有些人想取得伟人所获得并保持的成就，他们就必须不断运用自身才能，以便开启知识的大门，即那些通往人类努力探求的各个领域的大门，这些领域包括各种职业：科学、艺术、文学、农业等。

勤奋使开启成功宝库的钥匙保持光亮。如果休·米勒在采石场劳作一天后，晚上的时光用来休息消遣的话，他就不会成为名垂青史的地质学家。著名数学家爱德蒙·斯通如果闲暇时无所事事，就不会出版数学词典，也不会发现开启数学之门的钥匙。如果苏格兰青年弗格森在山坡上放羊时，让他那思维活跃的大脑处于休息

103

have found the key to science of **mathematics**, if he had given his spare moments to idleness, had the little Scotch lad, Ferguson, allowed the busy brain to go to sleep while he tended sheep on the hillside instead of **calculating** the position of the stars by a string of beads, he would never have become a famous astronomer.

Labor **vanquishes** all—not inconstant, spasmodic, or ill-directed labor; but faithful, unremitting, daily effort toward a well-directed purpose. Just as truly as eternal vigilance is the price of liberty, so is eternal industry the price of noble and enduring success.

状态，而不是借助一串珠子计算星星的位置，他就不会成为著名的天文学家。

劳动征服一切。这里所指的劳动不是断断续续的、间歇性的或方向偏差的劳动，而是坚定的、不懈的、方向正确的每日劳动。正如要想拥有自由就要时刻保持警惕一样，要想取得伟大的、持久的成功，就必须坚持不懈地努力。

单词解析 Word Analysis

inscription [ɪnˈskrɪpʃn] *n.* （作者）题词，献词
- The medal bears the inscription "For distinguished service".
  奖章上刻有"功勋卓越"的字样。

afflict [əˈflɪkt] *v.* 使受痛苦，折磨
- Italy has been afflicted by political corruption for decades.
  几十年来意大利一直饱受政治腐败之苦。

idleness [ˈaɪdlnəs] *n.* 懒惰；闲散；安逸；失业（状态）；无益；白费
- Idleness is a very bad thing for human nature.
  懒散是人性中很糟糕的一面。

industrious [ɪnˈdʌstriəs] *adj.* 勤勉的；勤奋的
- She was an industrious and willing worker.
  她是个勤劳肯干的员工。

If I Rest I Rust 如果我休息，我就会生锈 18

industry [ˈɪndəstri] *n.* 勤勉；勤奋；工业；行业

例 No one doubted his ability, his industry or his integrity.
没人怀疑他的能力、勤奋和正直。

British industry suffers through insufficient investment in research.
研究投入不足让英国工业深受其害。

treasury [ˈtreʒəri] *n.* （政府的）财政部

例 The Treasury has long been predicting an upturn in consumer spending.
财政部早就预测消费者支出会出现上扬。

recreation [ˌrekriˈeɪʃn] *n.* 娱乐

例 Saturday afternoon is for recreation and outings.
周六午后是休闲和外出游玩的时间。

mathematics [ˌmæθəˈmætɪks] *n.* 数学；数学运算；数学应用

例 Elizabeth studied mathematics and classics.
伊丽莎白学过数学和古典文学。

calculating [ˈkælkjuleɪtɪŋ] *adj.* 计算的；有算计的；慎重的

例 I believe I am capable of calculating the political consequences accurately.
我觉得我能准确预料此事的政治后果。

vanquish [ˈvæŋkwɪʃ] *v.* 克服

例 With knowledge and wisdom, evil could be vanquished on this earth.
拥有了知识和智慧就能够把恶势力从这个世界上铲除。

语法知识点 Grammar points

① The significant inscription found on an old key— "If I rest, I rust" —would be an excellent motto for those who are afflicted with the slightest bit of idleness.

105

be afflicted with 受折磨
> 例 They are always afflicted with the noise made by the passing planes.
> 他们经常被过往的飞机搅得不安宁。

② Those who would attain the heights reached and kept by great men must keep their faculties polished by constant use, so that they...

句子主干：Those must keep their faculties...；who引导定语从句；so that引导目的状语从句；entrances to..."通往……的入口"。

> 例 These crosses on the drawing designate all possible entrances to the castle.
> 图上的十字记号指出了城堡里所有可能的入口。
> Swaddle your newborn baby so that she feels secure.
> 把你刚出生的孩子用襁褓包裹住，这样她会有安全感。

③ Had the little Scotch lad, Ferguson, allowed the busy brain to go to sleep while he tended sheep on the hillside instead of calculating the position of the stars by a string of beads...

这句话是倒装句。主干是：Had the little Scotch... allowed the busy brain...，he would never have become a famous astronomer. 相当于if the little Scotch... allowed the busy brain... he would never have become a famous astronomer.

allow sb. /sth. to do 允许某人/某物做，被动语态是be allowed to do sth.

> 例 The children are not allowed to watch violent TV programmes.
> 儿童不准收看含暴力内容的电视节目。
> He won't allow himself to fail.
> 他不会任由自己失败的。

④ Just as truly as eternal vigilance is the price of liberty, so is eternal industry the price of noble and enduring success.

eternal vigilance 永久的警惕

> 例 The price of liberty is eternal vigilance.
> 自由的代价是永久提高警惕。

so+谓语+主语：……也一样，仅用于肯定句。

> 例 I know how much you love him. so does he.
> 我知道你有多爱他，他也一样。

If I Rest I Rust
如果我休息，我就会生锈

经典名句 Famous Classics

1. Business may be troublesome, but idleness is pernicious.
   事业虽扰人，怠惰害更大。

2. It is no honour for an eagle to vanquish a dove.
   以强凌弱，胜之不武。

3. Just as truly as eternal vigilance is the price of liberty, so is eternal industry the price of noble and enduring success.
   正如要想拥有自由就要时刻保持警惕一样，要想取得伟大的、持久的成功，就必须坚持不懈地努力。

4. Learn from yesterday, live for today, hope for tomorrow.
   学习昨天，活在今天，期待明天。

5. Success is how high you bounce when you hit bottom.
   成功与否取决于当你触底后反弹的高度。

6. It's easy to feel like you don't need help, but it's harder to walk on your own.
   我不需要任何人的帮助，这句话说起来容易，但是当你无依无靠的时候，往往走得很艰难。

7. Artificial intelligence is no match for natural stupidity.
   假装聪明还不如保持愚蠢。

8. The world belongs to the enthusiast who keeps cool.
   世界属于那些冷静的狂热分子。

9. Love the life you live, live the life you love.
   喜欢自己过的生活，过自己喜欢的生活。

10. Remember happiness doesn't depend upon who you are or what you have; it depends solely on what you think.
    幸福不在于你是谁，你拥有什么，而仅仅在于你自己怎么看待。

19 The Metal of Life
生活的奖牌

After giving a talk at a high school, I was asked to pay a visit to a special student. An illness had kept the boy home, but he had **expressed** an interest in meeting me, and it would mean a great deal to him. I agreed.

During the nine-mile drive to his home, I found out something about Matthew. He had **muscular dystrophy**. When he was born, the doctor told his parents that he would not live to see five, and then they were told he would not make it to ten. Now he was thirteen. He wanted to meet me because I was a gold-**medal lifter**, and I knew about **overcoming obstacles** and going for my dreams.

I spent over an hour talking to Matthew. Never once did he complain or ask, "why me?". He spoke about winning and succeeding and going for his dreams. **Obviously**, he knew what he was talking about. He didn't mention that his classmates had made fun of him because he was different. He just talked about his hopes for the future, and how one day he wanted to lift weights with me.

When we finished talking, I went

有一次我在高等学校做演讲，演讲完后，我被请求去见一个特殊的学生。疾病使这个男学生不得不待在家里，但是他非常想见我一面，因为这对他有非常重大的意义，于是我同意了。

我们驱车行驶9英里来到了马修的家里，在此期间我了解到他的一些情况。他有肌肉萎缩症。当他一出生的时候医生就告诉他的父母他活不到五岁，后来他们又被告知这个孩子不可能活到十岁，但是现在马修十三岁了，他想见我是因为我是一个金牌举重获得者，我懂得如何去克服困难和障碍去追寻梦想。

我和马修谈了一个多小时，但是他一次也没有抱怨过或问："为什么这种情况发生在我身上？"，他一直谈论着关于胜利和成功以及追求梦想的话题，很显然，他知道自己在讨论什么，他没有提他的同学因为他的不同而嘲笑他的事情，他只是在诉说着关于对未来的憧憬，希望有一天他像我

The Metal of Life
生活的奖牌

to my **briefcase** and pulled out the first medal I won and put it around his neck. I told him he was more of a winner and knew more about success and overcoming obstacles than I ever would. He looked at it for a moment, and then took it off and handed back it to me, he said, "You are a **champion**. You earned that medal. Someday when I get to the Olympics and win my own medals, I will show it to you."

Last summer I received a letter from Matthew's parents telling me that Matthew had passed away. They wanted me to have a letter he had written to me a few days before.

Dear Rick,

My Mum said I should send you a thank-you letter for your talking with me. I also want to let you know that the doctors tell me that I don't have long to live any more. But I still smile as much as I can.

I told you someday I was going to the **Olympics** and win a gold medal. But I know now I will never to get to do that. But I know I'm a champion, and God knows that too. When I get to Heaven, God will give me my medal and when you get there, I will show it to you.

Thank you for loving me.
Yours friend,
Matthew

一样去举重。

当我们完成这次交谈时，我从公文包里拿出我第一次赢得的金奖牌戴在他的脖子上，我告诉他，他比一个冠军更厉害，比我更有能力去克服困难赢得成功。他看了看这块金牌然后摘下它还给了我，他说："你是一个冠军，是你赢得了这块奖牌，有一天我也会去参加奥林匹克然后赢得属于我自己的奖牌，我会给你看的。"

去年夏天我得到了马修已经去世的消息和一封几天前马修写给我的信。

亲爱的瑞克：

我妈妈说我应该给你写一封信感谢你寄给我的照片，医生说我恐怕活不了多久了，但是我仍然尽可能地微笑着面对这一切。

我曾经告诉过你有一天我会参加奥林匹克然后去赢得我的金牌，但是我现在知道我将永远也不会得到它了，但是我知道我仍然是一个冠军，上帝也知道我是，我到了天堂的时候，上帝将会给我那枚奖牌，那么当你去的时候，我一定会给你看的。

谢谢你对我的爱
你的朋友
马修

单词解析 *Word Analysis*

express [ɪk'spres] *v.* 表达，表示
- We can express that equation like that.
  我们可以这样表示那个等式。

muscular dystrophy *n.* 肌肉萎缩症
- She was the poster child for muscular dystrophy.
  她是海报上那个患肌肉萎缩的小孩。

medal ['medl] *n.* 奖牌
- It was an unbelievable moment when Chris won the gold medal.
  克里斯赢得金牌的那一刻令人不可思议。

lifter ['lɪftə] *n.* 举重运动员
- He looks much too skinny / scrawny to be a weight-lifter.
  他瘦骨嶙峋的，当不了举重运动员。

overcome [ˌəʊvə'kʌm] *v.* 克服
- Find a way to overcome your difficulties.
  找出办法战胜困难。

obstacle ['ɒbstəkl] *n.* 障碍，困难；障碍物
- Overcrowding remains a large obstacle to improving conditions.
  过分拥挤仍然是改善环境的一大障碍。
- Most competition cars will only roll over if they hit an obstacle.
  大多数赛车只有在撞上障碍物时才会翻车。

obviously ['ɒbviəsli] *adv.* 明显地
- They obviously appreciate you very much.
  他们显然对你十分感激。

briefcase ['briːfkeɪs] *n.* 公文包
- He packed a briefcase with what might be required.
  他把所有可能需要的东西都装进公文包。

champion ['tʃæmpiən] *n.* 冠军；支持者；拥护者；捍卫者

The Metal of Life 生活的奖牌 19

例 Kasparov became world champion.
卡斯帕罗夫成为世界冠军。
He was once known as a champion of social reform.
他曾经是社会改革的拥护者。

Olympics [əʊˈlɪmpɪks] *n.* 奥林匹克运动会的（Olympic的名词复数）

例 She won the individual gold medal at the Winter Olympics.
她在冬奥会上获得了个人金牌。

语法知识点 Grammar points

① **After giving a talk at a high school, I was asked to pay a visit to a special student.**

pay a visit to 去参观，拜访

例 We pay a yearly visit to my uncle.
我们每年都要看望我的叔叔。

② **An illness had kept the boy home, but he had expressed an interest in meeting me, and it would mean a great deal to him.**

mean a great deal to sb 对某人意义很大

例 Your friendship means a great deal to me.
你的友谊对我极为珍贵。

③ **Last summer I received a letter from Matthew's parents telling me that Matthew had passed away. They wanted me to have a letter he had written to me a few days before.**

pass away 去世；（时间等）消磨掉

例 He unfortunately passed away last year.
他去年不幸逝世。
In it the Indians pass away hot noon hours, napping or chatting.
印第安人躺在上面，时而小憩时而闲聊，打发掉了正午几个小时的酷热。

④ **I also want to let you know that the doctors tell me that I don't have long to live anymore.**

两个that引导两个宾语从句，that可省略。

not... any more不再,通常情况下可以和not... any longer互换,相当于no more/no longer。

例 She used to study English, but she doesn't study it any longer/any more.

她以前学英语的,但是现在不再学了。

You can drink no more. = You can't drink any more.

你不能再喝了。

注意:no longer/no more本身就带有否定含义,表示"再也不",所以不能在同一个句子中加入否定词。

经典名句 *Famous Classics*

1. We wish genius and morality were affectionate companions, but it is a fact that they are often bitter enemies.
   我们希望天分与美德能够相处融洽,但是实际情况是它们经常互为劲敌。

2. The omission of good is no less reprehensible than the commission of evil.
   对善行的忽视不亚于犯下罪行。

3. I'll tell you a big secret, my friend: Don't wait for the Last Judgement. It happens everyday.
   我要告诉你一个巨大的秘密,朋友,别再等最终审判了,它每天都在发生。

4. I would remind you that extremism in the defence of liberty is no vice! And let me remind you also that moderation in the pursuit of justice is no virtue!
   我要提醒你们,捍卫自由时得极端并不是罪恶!我也要提醒你们,追求正义时的温和绝非道德!

5. How far that little candle throws his beams! So shines a good deed in a naughty world.
   这根小小的蜡烛,它的光芒投射得多么远啊!就像是美德在这个荒芜的世界里发出的光芒一样。

The Metal of Life 生活的奖牌 19

6. The true hypocrite is the one who ceases to perceive his deception, the one who lies with sincerity.
   真正的伪君子是那些已经意识不到自己的谎言的人，那些真诚地欺骗着别人的人。

7. It is necessary to the happiness of man that he be mentally faithful to himself. Infidelity does not consist in believing, or in disbelieving, it consists in professing to believe what one does not believe.
   对自己忠诚是得到幸福的必须。背信并非在于简单的相信与否，而是假装相信自己不相信的东西。

8. Nice guys, when we turn nasty, can make a terrible mess of it, usually because we've had so little practice, and have bottled it up for too long.
   好人堕落的时候会十分糟糕，一半是因为他们缺乏这方面的练习，另一半则是因为压抑了太久。

读书笔记

20 Rules of Credibility
诚信的规则

Progressive future and successful life require **discipline** and character. These things are **embedded** into the pattern of our lives through proper education and interaction with fellow human beings. A solid foundation of time tested nurtured values attach a character to each and every one of us. Finally, wherever we go we carry our character sub-consciously with us.

A person is character **personified** only if he has enough credibility. Credibility is an essential attribute that is built on the elements of integrity, reliability, veracity, competence and commitment. Credibility shines in those people who are ethically motivated. Credibility is an important tool in improving your people skills. Credibility ensures a person to win the genuine respect, confidence and trust of others. To build up enough credibility we have to have a gel of following elements.

Integrity: In simple words it means standing for your values and be firm on your view. Integrity is an essential factor to win the adulation and trust of others. Integrity is the **solidarity** with which

进步的未来和成功的生活需要纪律和个人的品质。他们通过教育与其他人的互动耕植于我们的生活方式中。久经考验的价值观奠定的坚实的基础赋予每一个人的品质。最后，无论我们走到哪里，我们身上都会潜意识地随时反映我们的品质。

如果有足够的诚信，品质就会个性化。诚信是一个基本的特质，是建立在正直、可靠、诚实、能力和承诺的基础上崇高道德的人身上发出的光芒。诚信是可以提高你做人的技巧的。诚信使人获得由衷的敬意、自信和别人的信任。要建立足够的诚信，我们必须拥有以下的品质。

正直：简单而言，它捍卫你的价值观和坚定你的观点。正直使你得到别人的崇敬和信任。正直使人们无法无视你的存在。

可靠性：可靠性是培养相互信任和提升人际关系的基础。可靠性反映在我们和别人的沟通，对他人承诺和陈述的

you make your presence felt.

Reliability: **Reliability** is a very addictive breeding ground for mutual trust and improved interpersonal relations. Evidence of reliability lies in the **consistency** with which we deliver on **commitment**, promises and statements.

Competence: Competence is the combined effort of knowledge application, experience and **conscientious** effort to the best possible solution for a given problem. When **deadlines** have to be met at the earliest a person's competence is the only handy tool that will see him through that deadline. A competent person has no ifs and buts in his vocabulary. He won't fix a blame for failure on something or someone, but will modulate himself to rectify the situation.

Commitment: A proper canalization of one's energy, **enthusiasm**, talent and thoughts into completing a given project or thoughts is commitment. Commitment calls in for a firm mental resolve to fulfill the job at hand and see it through. A committed person won't rest on his **laurels** till he has completed his duty.

No one is born perfect. But one can hone one's skills by being true to oneself. Early realization of the important change in your life can take you places. So be far sighted and yes do let me know the results.

一致性。

能力：能力是知识应用、经验和认真应对解决问题的综合表现。个人的能力是有助于到达期限目的的唯一方便工具。有能力的人的字典里没有"如果"和"但是"，他们不会为失败而谴责其他的人和事，他们将调整自己去改变处境。

承诺：正确投入个人的能量、热情、才能和思考去完成一个项目和一个想法是承诺。承诺需要坚定的决心去完成手头的工作。一个守承诺的人不完成任务是不会言休的。

没有人生来是完美的，但可以通过坦诚对待自己来不断地磨炼自己。早些意识到生活中的重要变化，会使你所向披靡。因此保持远见，并告诉我结果如何。

单词解析 *Word Analysis*

discipline [ˈdɪsəplɪn] *n.* 符合行为准则的行为（或举止）

例 It was that image of calm and discipline that appealed to voters.
正是那个冷静、自律的形象打动了选民。

embed [ɪmˈbed] *v.* 把……嵌入，埋入

例 One of the bullets passed through Andrea's chest before embedding itself in a wall.
其中一颗子弹射穿了安德烈亚的胸部，打入一面墙中。

personify [pəˈsɒnɪfaɪ] *v.* 将（某事物）人格化、拟人化

例 The personify the divine and magic powers worshipped by the people.
它们把人们崇拜的神力和魔力都人格化了。

solidarity [ˌsɒlɪˈdærəti] *n.* 团结

例 The solidarity among China's various nationalities is as firm as a rock.
中国各族人民之间的团结坚如磐石。

reliability [rɪˌlaɪəˈbɪləti] *n.* 可靠，可信赖

例 He's not at all worried about his car's reliability.
对于自己那台车性能的稳定性他根本不担心。

consistency [kənˈsɪstənsi] *n.* 连贯；符合；前后一致；稠度

例 There's always a lack of consistency in matters of foreign policy.
外交政策总是缺乏连贯性。
I added a little milk to mix the dough to the right consistency.
我加了一点儿牛奶，好让面团稠度适中。

commitment [kəˈmɪtmənt] *n.* 承诺，许诺；委任，委托；责任

例 We made a commitment to keep working together.
我们承诺继续合作。
Work commitments forced her to uproot herself and her son from Reykjavik.

Rules of Credibility 20
诚信的规则

她的工作迫使她和儿子从雷克雅未克搬走。

competence [ˈkɒmpɪtəns] *n.* 能力，技能

例 We've always regarded him as a man of integrity and high professional competence.
我们一直都认为他是个正直而且业务能力很强的人。

conscientious [ˌkɒnʃɪˈenʃəs] *adj.* 认真的，勤奋的

例 Virginia was still struggling to be a conscientious and dedicated mother.
弗吉尼亚还在尽力成为一位勤勤恳恳、全心奉献的母亲。

deadlines [ˈdedlaɪnz] *n.* 最后期限（deadline的名词复数）

例 This gives you more self-esteem and more reasonable deadlines.
这会赋予你更多自尊和更多合理的期限。

enthusiasm [ɪnˈθjuːziæzəm] *n.* 热情；热心，热忱

例 Their skill, enthusiasm and running has got them in the team.
他们的技术、热忱和跑动能力使他们得以加入这支球队。
Draw him out about his current enthusiasms and future plans.
让他畅所欲言地谈谈自己目前热衷的活动和将来的计划。

laurels [ˈlɒrəlz] *n.* 荣誉，胜利，名声

例 The resourceful jurist formed a plan to recover his own laurels.
足智多谋的法学家想出了一个恢复名誉的计策。

语法知识点 Grammar points

① Credibility ensures a person to win the genuine respect, confidence and trust of others. To build up enough credibility we have to have a gel of following elements.

build up 逐步建立；增进

例 The delegations had begun to build up some trust in one another.
代表团彼此之间开始建立了些许信任。

Exercise in pregnancy can build up your strength and suppleness.
孕期锻炼身体可以增强体力和柔韧性。

② **In simple words it means standing for your values and be firm on your view.**

mean doing 意味着

例 Pushing or pulling, however, does not necessarily mean doing work.
然而，推或拉未必意味着做功。

③ **Evidence of reliability lies in the consistency with which we deliver on commitment, promises and statements.**

句中with+which引导的是定语从句。

lie in 在于

例 All their hopes lie in him.
他们把所有希望都寄托在他身上。

④ **So be far sighted and yes, do let me know the results.**

sight在此句中是"远见"之意，注意与其搭配：have long (far) sight远视；有远见。short (near) sight近视；缺乏远见。catch sight of 看见。

例 Every time I catch sight of myself in the mirror, I feel so disappointed.
每次我瞥见镜子里的自己就觉得沮丧。

Only a short-sighted man will lose sight of the importance of education.
只有鼠目寸光的人才会看不见教育的重要性。

经典名句 *Famous Classics*

1. No one is born perfect. But one can hone one's skills by being true to oneself.
   没有人生来是完美的，但可以通过坦诚对待自己来不断地磨炼自己。

2. Desire persuades me one way, reason another. I see the better and approve it, but I follow the worse.
   欲望将我引向一方，理智将我领向另一方。我看到正确的方向，并且表示赞同，然后走向错误的那一方。

3. The fact that man knows right from wrong proves his intellectual superiority to the other creatures; but the fact that he can do

Rules of Credibility
诚信的规则 20

wrong proves his moral inferiority to any creatures that cannot.
人类能够分辨是非，这说明他在智慧上超越其他生物；但人类会做错事，又说明他在道德上比不会犯错的动物更为低等。

4. Science without religion is lame, religion without science is blind.
没有信仰的科学是很蹩脚的，没有科学的信仰又是盲目的。

5. Vulgarity has its uses. Vulgarity often cuts ice which refinement scrapes at vainly.
粗俗也有其功用。当那些优雅高贵的人徒劳地挠来挠去的时候，粗俗之人能够劈开冰面。

6. There are some men who turn a deaf ear to reason and good advice, and willfully go wrong for fear of being controlled.
有些人仅仅为了怕受人控制，就对忠言良策充耳不闻，甚至故意犯错。

7. There are different ways of assassinating a man—by pistol, sword, poison, or moral assassination. They are the same in their results except that the last is more cruel.
杀一个人有许多方法——手枪，刀剑，毒药或者道德上的攻击。它们的效果大抵相同，而最后一种尤为残忍。

8. The safest road to Hell is the gradual one—the gentle slope, soft underfoot, without sudden turnings, without milestones, without signposts.
通向地狱的道路是平缓的，踩上去很柔软，没有急转弯，没有里程碑，也没有路标。

9. When nature exceeds culture, we have the rustic. When culture exceeds nature, we have the pedant.
质胜文则野，文胜质则史。

10. We have erred, and strayed from thy ways like lost sheep. We have followed too much the devices and desires of our own hearts.
我们犯下错误，脱离正道就像迷途的羔羊。我们过分听从了内心的狡诈和欲望。

11. Emancipate yourself from your past. The only way to move forward is to stop looking back!
把自己从过去解放出来，前进的唯一方法是别往后看。

21 A Good Heart to Lean On
善心可依

When I was growing up, I was embarrassed to be seen with my father. He was severely **crippled** and very short, and when we would walk together, his hand on my arm for balance, people would stare. I would **inwardly squirm** at the unwanted attention. If he ever noticed or was bothered, he never let on.

It was difficult to **coordinate** our steps—his halting, mine impatient—and because of that, we didn't say much as we went along. But as we started out, he always said, "You set the pace. I will try to adjust to you."

Our usual walk was to or from the subway, which was how he got to work. He went to work sick, and despite **nasty** weather. He almost never missed a day, and would make it to the office even if others could not. A matter of pride.

When snow or ice was on the ground, it was impossible for him to walk, even with help. At such times my sisters or I would pull him through the streets of Brooklyn, NY, on a child's sleigh to the subway entrance. Once there, he would cling to the **handrail** until he reached the lower steps that

在我成长的过程中，我一直羞于让别人看见我和父亲在一起。我的父亲身材矮小，腿上有严重的残疾。当我们一起走路时，他总是挽着我以保持身体平衡，这时总招来一些异样的目光，令我无地自容。可是如果他注意到了这些，不管他内心多么痛苦，也从不表现出来。

走路时，我们很难相互协调——他的步子慢慢腾腾，我的步子焦躁不安。所以一路上我们交谈得很少。但是每次出行前，他总是说，"你走你的，我想法儿跟上你。"

我们常常往返于从家到他上班乘坐的地铁站的那段路上。他有病也要上班，哪怕天气恶劣。他几乎从未误过一天工，就是在别人不能去的情况下，他也要设法去上班。实在值得骄傲！

每当冰封大地、雪花飘飘的时候，若是没有帮助，他简直举步维艰。每当此时，我或我的姐妹们就用儿童雪橇把他拉过纽约布鲁克林区的街道，一直送他到地铁的入口处。一到那儿，他便手抓扶手一直走

the warmer tunnel air kept ice-free. In Manhattan the subway station was the basement of his office building, and he would not have to go outside again until we met him in Brooklyn on his way home.

When I think of it now, **I marvel** at how much courage it must have taken for a grown man to subject himself to such **indignity** and stress. And at how he did it—without bitterness or complaint.

On one memorable occasion a fight broke out at a beach party, with everyone **punching** and **shoving**. He wasn't **content** to sit and watch, but he couldn't stand unaided on the soft sand. In frustration he began to shout, "I'll fight anyone who will tit down with me!" Nobody did. But the next day people kidded him by saying it was the first time any fighter was urged to take a dive even before the bout began.

I now know he participated in some things **vicariously** through me, his only son. When I played ball (poorly), he "played" too. When I joined the Navy he "joined" too. And when I came home on leave, he saw to it that I visited his office. Introducing me, he was really saying, "This is my son, but it is also me, and I could have done this, too, if

到底下的台阶时才放开手，因为那里通道的空气暖和些，地面上没有结冰。到了曼哈顿，地铁站就在他办公楼的地下一层，在我们在布鲁克林接他回家之前他无须再走出楼来。

如今每当我想起这些，我惊叹一个成年男子要经受这种侮辱和压力得需要多么大的勇气啊！叹服他竟然能够做到这一点，不带任何痛苦，没有丝毫抱怨。

记得有一次海边晚会上，有人打架，动了拳头，推推搡搡。他不甘于坐在那里当观众，但又无法在松软的沙滩上自己站起来。于是，失望之下，他吼了起来："谁想坐下和我打？"没有人响应。但是第二天，人们都取笑他说比赛还没开始，拳击手就被劝认输，这还是头一次看见。

现在我知道一些事情他是通过我——他唯一的儿子来做的。当我打球时（尽管我打得很差），他也在"打球"。当我参加海军时，他也"参加"。当我回家休息时，他一定要让我去他的办公室，在介绍我时，他真真切切地说："这是我儿子，但也是我自己，假如事情不是这样的话，

things had been different."

He has been gone many years now, but I think of him often. I wonder if he sensed my reluctance to be seen with him during our walks. If he did, I am sorry I never told him how sorry I was, how unworthy I was, how I regretted it. I think of him when I complain about trifles, when I am **envious** of another's good fortune, when I don't have a "good heart".

我也会去参军的。"

父亲离开我们已经很多年了,但是我时常想起他。我不知道他是否意识到我曾经不愿意让人看到和他走在一起的心理。假如他知道这一切,我现在感到很遗憾,因为我从没告诉过他我是多么愧疚、多么不孝、多么悔恨。每当我为一些琐事而抱怨时,为别人的好运而妒忌时,我觉得自己缺乏"善心"时,我就会想起我的父亲。

单词解析 Word Analysis

cripple ['krɪpl] v. 使残疾,损害 n. 瘸子;残疾人

例 He had been warned that another bad fall could cripple him for life.
医生警告他,如果再次严重摔伤他可能会终身残疾。
She has gone from being a healthy, fit, and sporty young woman to being a cripple.
她从一个健康、强壮、爱好运动的年轻女性变成了一个跛子。

inwardly ['ɪnwədli] adv. 在内心

例 He pretended to be affronted, but inwardly he was pleased.
他假装受到了冒犯,但其实内心很高兴。

squirm [skwɜːm] v. 蠕动,扭动

例 She squirmed out of his arms.
她扭动着挣脱了他的拥抱。

coordinate [kəʊˈɔːdɪneɪt] v. (使)配合

例 She'll show you how to co-ordinate pattern and colours.
她会教您如何搭配款式和颜色。

A Good Heart to Lean On
善心可依

nasty ['nɑːsti] *adj.* 肮脏的，不愉快的
- Though he had a temper and could be nasty, it never lasted.
  虽然他爱发脾气，而且有时还很讨厌，但向来都只是一阵儿。
  That is Emily's nasty little house in Balham.
  那是埃米莉在巴勒姆的脏乱小屋。

sleigh [sleɪ] *n.* 雪橇
- The sleigh was on one runner, heeling like a yacht in a wind.
  这架雪橇在一根滑橇上滑行，倾斜得像大风中的一艘快艇。

handrail ['hændreɪl] *n.* （楼梯）扶手
- When travelling at bus or metro, please hold the handrail.
  坐公交或地铁时，请抓紧扶手。

marvel ['mɑːvl] *v.* 诧异
- Her fellow members marveled at her seemingly infinite energy.
  她的同事们对她似乎无穷的精力大为惊叹。

indignity [ɪn'dɪɡnəti] *n.* 轻蔑，侮辱
- Later, he suffered the indignity of having to flee angry protesters.
  后来，他不得不极不光彩地避开愤怒的抗议者溜走了。

punch [pʌntʃ] *v.* （用拳头）猛砸
- After punching him on the chin she wound up hitting him over the head.
  她先挥拳打他的下巴，然后又打他的脑袋。

shove [ʃʌv] *v.* 推，乱推
- He was then shoved face down on the pavement.
  接着他被一把推倒，脸朝下趴在了人行道上。

content ['kɒntent] *adj.* 满意的 *n.* 含量
- Sunflower margarine has the same fat content as butter.
  向日葵所制人造黄油的脂肪含量与黄油脂肪含量相同。
  I am content to admire the mountains from below.
  我满足于从山脚下观赏山景。

我的人生美文：那些随风飘逝的日子

vicariously [vɪˈkeərɪəslɪ] *adv.* 可替代地，间接感受到地

例 By observation of one type and another I gathered experience vicariously.
通过种种观察我间接地获得了经验。

envious [ˈenvɪəs] *adj.* 妒忌的

例 I don't think I'm envious of your success.
我想我并不嫉妒你的成功。

语法知识点 Grammar points

① "You set the pace, I will try to adjust to you."

句中pace 原意指（在赛跑中）领先定步调；（在文中可理解为比喻意）立下生活等之榜样。
adjust to 调整，使适合于

例 Foreigners take some time to adjust to our way of life.
外国人要花一些时间才能适应我们的生活方式。

② Once there, he would cling to the handrail until he reached the lower steps that the warmer tunnel air kept ice-free.

然后他就紧抓着铁道通口的扶手，直到下面没有冰雪的台阶才放手。
句中cling to意思是抓紧（某物）；ice-free（原指港口）不冻的，此处指地铁下面无积雪。

例 The birds cling to the wall and nibble at the brickwork.
鸟儿们紧贴在墙上，啄着砖缝。

③ I marvel at how much courage it must have taken for a grown man to subject himself to such indignity and stress.

我感到十分惊叹，像他那么一个年长的人，得有多大的勇气才能屈就这样的窘境。
句中marvel at意思是（对……）感到惊叹；subject himself to意思是使遭受；使经历。

例 No one would willingly subject himself to such indignities.
没有人愿意使自己蒙受如此的侮辱。

A Good Heart to Lean On
善心可依 21

经典名句 Famous Classics

1. Haters never win. I just think that's true about life, because negative energy always costs in the end.
   愤恨的人永远无法取得胜利。我认为这是生活的真理,因为负面的情绪总会产生代价。

2. Moral principles please our minds as beef and mutton and pork please our mouths.
   理义之悦我心,犹刍豢之悦我口。(理义能够让我愉悦,就像是牛羊肉让我觉得美味一样。)

3. Recommend virtue to your children; it alone, not money, can make them happy. I speak from experience.
   把美德推荐给孩子们吧,只有美德而非金钱才能让他们幸福。这是我的经验之谈。

4. Absolute truth is a very rare and dangerous commodity in the context of professional journalism.
   绝对的真理在记者职业中,是极为罕见也极为危险的东西。

5. We must not indulge in unfavorable views of mankind, since by doing it we make bad men believe they are no worse than others, and we teach the good that they are good in vain.
   我们不能沉浸在对人类的失望之中,因为这样会让恶劣的人觉得自己不比别人更坏,而善良的人会觉得自己没有必要做个好人。

6. Pride, envy, and avarice are the three sparks that have set these hearts on fire.
   骄傲、妒忌和贪婪是让心灵起火的三大火苗。

7. To vilify a great man is the readiest way in which a little man can himself attain greatness.
   小人往往喜欢诽谤伟人们,这让他们觉得自己某种意义上也变得伟大起来。

8. In America everybody is of opinion that he has no social superiors, since all men are equal, but he does not admit that he has no social inferiors.
   在美国,人们不承认有比自己高等的社会阶级,因为人生而平等;但他们并不否认有低于自己的等级。

125

22 The Gold in the Orchard
果园里的金子

There was once a farmer who had a fine **olive orchard**. He was very hardworking, and the farm always **prospered** under his care. But he knew that his three sons **despised** the farm work, and were eager to make wealth through **adventure**.

When the farmer was old, and felt that his time had come to an end, he called the three sons to him and said, "My sons, there is a **pot** of gold hidden in the olive orchard. Dig for it, if you wish it."

The sons tried to get him to tell them in what part of the orchard the gold was hidden; but he would tell them nothing more.

After the farmer was dead, the sons went to work to find the pot of gold; since they did not know where the hiding-place was, they agreed to begin in a line, at one end of the orchard, and to dig until one of them should find the money.

They dug until they had turned up the soil from one end of the orchard to the other, round the tree-roots and between them. But no pot of gold was to be found. It seemed as if someone must have stolen it, or as if the farmer had been **wandering** in his **wits**. The

从前有一个农民，他有一座漂亮的橄榄园。他非常勤劳，而且农场在他的照管下蒸蒸日上。可他知道自己的三个儿子瞧不起农活，都迫不及待地想通过冒险发家致富。

这个农民上了年岁，感到死期快要来临时，将三个儿子叫到身边说："儿子们，橄榄园里藏有一罐金子。你们想要，就去挖吧。"

儿子们想让父亲告诉他们金子藏在果园的哪一块地方，可他什么也没再跟他们说。

那个农民死后，三个儿子就开始挖地，想找到那罐金子；因为他们不知道金子藏在什么地方，所以他们一致同意排成一行从果园的一头开始挖起，直到其中一人挖到金子为止。

他们挖啊挖，从果园的一头一直挖到了另一头，果树周围和果树之间也都挖了，可还是没有找到那罐金子。看来一定是有人已经把那罐金子偷走了，要么就是他们的父亲一直在异想天开。三个儿子对他们白干了一场感到大失所望。

到了第二年的橄榄季节，

The Gold in the Orchard 果园里的金子 22

three sons were **bitterly disappointed** to have all their work for nothing.

The next olive season, the olive trees in the orchard bore more fruit than they had ever given; when it was sold, it gave the sons a whole pot of gold.

And when they saw how much money had come from the orchard, they suddenly understood what the wise father had meant when he said, "There is gold hidden in the orchard. Dig for it, if you wish it."

果园里的橄榄树接出的果子比以往的都多。卖完果子后，三个儿子赚了整整一罐金子。

他们从果园里得到这么多钱后，突然明白了聪明的父亲所说的"果园里藏有金子，想要就去挖吧"这句话的含义。

单词解析 Word Analysis

olive ['ɒlɪv] *n.* 橄榄；橄榄树；橄榄色 *adj.* 橄榄色的；黄褐色的；淡褐色的；橄榄绿的

例 He had a strong Greek nose and olive-black eyes.
他有一个高挺的希腊式鼻子和一双墨橄榄绿色的眼睛。
Olives look romantic on a hillside in Provence.
普罗旺斯一处山坡上的橄榄林呈现出一派浪漫风情。

orchard ['ɔːtʃəd] *n.* 果园；果树林

例 Until his death in 1986 Greenwood owned and operated an enormous pear orchard.
到他1986年去世前，格林伍德一直拥有并管理着一片面积广阔的梨园。

prosper ['prɒspə(r)] *v.* 成功；繁荣，昌盛

例 The high street banks continue to prosper.
商业街上的银行仍旧一派繁荣景象。

despise [dɪ'spaɪz] *v.* 轻视，鄙视

例 I can never, ever forgive him. I despise him.
我永远不会原谅他，我鄙视他。

adventure [əd'ventʃə(r)] *n.* 冒险活动
> They're written as adventure stories. They're not intended to be deep.
> 它们是作为历险故事来写的，并没打算追求深刻。

pot [pɒt] *n.* 罐；壶；盆 *vt.* 把……栽入盆中
> Why not throw it all in the pot and see what happens?
> 为什么不把它全扔进罐子，看看会发生什么变化？
> Pot the cuttings individually.
> 把插条分别栽入盆中。

wander ['wɒndə(r)] *v.* 胡思乱想；游荡，漫游，闲逛
> They wandered off in the direction of the nearest store.
> 他们信步朝最近的商店走去。
> His mind would wander, and he would lose track of what he was doing.
> 他会走神，忘了自己正在干什么。

wit [wɪt] *n.* 智力；才智；智慧
> The information is there and waiting to be accessed by anyone with the wit to use it.
> 资料就摆在那儿，等着有头脑的人去利用。
> They love her practical attitude to life, her zest and wit.
> 他们喜欢她务实的人生态度、她的热情和幽默。

bitterly ['bɪtəli] *adj.* 悲痛地；苦涩地；怨恨地；残酷地
> We are bitterly upset at what has happened.
> 发生的事情让我们极为心烦。
> It was bitterly cold now and the ground was frozen hard.
> 现在天气冷极了，地面都冻硬了。

disappointed [ˌdɪsə'pɔɪntɪd] *adj.* 失望的，沮丧的
> When things go wrong, all of us naturally feel disappointed and frustrated.
> 出问题时，我们大家自然都感到失望和沮丧。

The Gold in the Orchard 果园里的金子 22

语法知识点 Grammar points

① **But he knew that his three sons despised the farm work, and were eager to make wealth through adventure.**

be eager to do 渴望做某事

例 I believe that you shouldn't be eager to find out a secret. It could change your life forever.
我认为，你不应该急于寻找一个秘密，它可以永远地改变你的生活。
He can be working hard under pressure and is eager to challenge new things.
他勇于承担工作压力，并愿意接受挑战。

② **The sons tried to get him to tell them in what part of the orchard the gold was hidden; but he would tell them nothing more.**

此句中 get sb. to do sth. = make sb. do sth. 使某人做某事

例 The boy made the girl cry.
男孩把女孩弄哭了。

③ **They dug until they had turned up the soil from one end of the orchard to the other, round the tree-roots and between them.**

turn up 出现；发生；开大；发现；卷起；使仰卧。在该句中为"出现"的意思。

例 You never know where happiness will turn up next.
你永远无法知道何时幸福会再次出现。

turn up 还可以表示"开大、调高（收音机、暖气等）"。

例 Bill would turn up the TV in the other room.
比尔会把另一个房间里的电视声音开大。

④ **It seemed as if someone must have stolen it, or as if the farmer had been wandering in his wits.**

seem as if 看上去好像

例 Julio Cesar made it seem as if we were playing with 11 men.
塞萨尔做得很出色，他让我们好像有11个人在比赛一样。

129

经典名句 Famous Classics

1. A modest man will not make a parade of his wealth.
   谦虚的人不会炫耀自己的财富。

2. Wealth make many friends; but the poor man is separated from his neighbor.
   富贵广交天下友，贫穷近邻不往来。

3. Knowledge make one laugh, but wealth make one dance.
   知识使人笑口常开，财富使人手舞足蹈。

4. Our greatest pretenses are built up not to hide the evil and the ugly in us, but our emptiness. The hardest thing to hide is something that is not there.
   我们最大程度的伪装不在于掩饰罪恶或丑陋，而是我们的空虚。根本不存在的东西最难掩盖。

5. The distinction between the past, present and future is only an illusion, however persistent.
   过去、现在和未来的差异不过是一个幻觉，然而这种幻觉顽固持久。

6. It's not that I'm afraid to die. I just don't want to be there when it happens.
   我不是害怕死亡，我只是不想到时候在场。

7. People often say that this or that person has not yet found himself. But the self is not something that one finds. It is something that one creates.
   人们总是说一个人"还没有找到自我"，但是自我不是要我们去寻找的，而是要我们去塑造的。

8. Any man's death diminishes me, because I am involved in Mankind; and therefore never send to know for whom the bell tolls; it tolls for thee.
   每个人的死去都使我更加衰弱，因为我是人类中的一分子；所以不要派人去问丧钟为谁而鸣；丧钟为你而鸣。

9. At eighteen our convictions are hills from which we look; at

forty-five they are caves in which we hide.

十八岁的时候信仰是我们所仰视的山峰，而四十五岁时信仰是我们所处的洞穴。

10. Nothing begins, and nothing ends. That is not paid with moan. For we are born in other's pain. And perish in our own.

一切的开始与结束，都以痛苦的呻吟为代价；因为我们在别人的痛苦中出生，在自己的痛苦中死亡。

23 Companionship of Books
以书为伴

A man may usually be known by the books he reads as well as by the company he keeps; for there is a **companionship** of books as well as of men; and one should always live in the best company, whether it be of books or of men.

A good book may be among the best of friends. It is the same today that it always was, and it will never change. It is the most patient and cheerful of companions. It does not turn its back upon us in times of adversity or distress. It always receives us with the same kindness; amusing and instructing us in youth, and comforting and **consoling** us in age.

Men often discover their **affinity** to each other by the mutual love they have for a book just as two persons sometimes discover a friend by the **admiration** which both entertain for a third. There is an old proverb, "Love me, love my dog." But there is more wisdom in this: "Love me, love my book." The book is a truer and higher bond of union. Men can think, feel, and sympathize with each other through their favorite author. They live in him together, and he in them.

通常看一个人读些什么书就可知道他的为人，就像看他同什么人交往就可知道他的为人一样，因为有人以人为伴，也有人以书为伴。无论是书友还是朋友，我们都应该以最好的为伴。

好书就像是你最好的朋友。它始终不渝，过去如此，现在如此，将来也永远不变。它是最有耐心、最令人愉悦的伴侣。在我们穷困潦倒、临危遭难时，它也不会抛弃我们，对我们总是一如既往地亲切。在我们年轻时，好书陶冶我们的性情，增长我们的知识；到我们年老时，它又给我们以慰藉和勉励。

人们常常因为喜欢同一本书而结为知己，就像有时两个人因为敬慕同一个人而成为朋友一样。有句古谚说："爱屋及乌。"其实"爱我及书"这句话蕴涵更多的哲理。书是更为真诚而高尚的情谊纽带。人们可以通过共同喜爱的作家沟通思想，交流感情，彼此息息相通，并与自己喜欢的作家思

Companionship of Books
以书为伴

A good book is often the best **urn** of a life **enshrining** the best that life could think out; for the world of a man's life is, for the most part, but the world of his thoughts. Thus the best books are **treasuries** of good words, the golden thoughts, which, remembered and cherished, become our constant companions and comforters.

Books possess an essence of **immortality**. They are by far the most lasting products of human effort. Temples and statues decay, but books survive. Time is of no account with great thoughts, which are as fresh today as when they first passed through their author's minds, ages ago. What was then said and thought still speaks to us as vividly as ever from the printed page. The only effect of time have been to sift out the bad products; for nothing in literature can long survive but what is really good.

Books introduce us into the best society; they bring us into the presence of the greatest minds that have ever lived. We hear what they said and did; we see them as if they were really alive; we sympathize with them, enjoy with them, grieve with them; their experience becomes ours, and we feel as if we were in a measure actors with them in the scenes which they describe.

The great and good do not die, even

想相通，情感相融。

好书常如最精美的宝器，珍藏着人生的思想的精华，因为人生的境界主要就在于其思想的境界。因此，最好的书是金玉良言和崇高思想的宝库，这些良言和思想若铭于心并多加珍视，就会成为我们忠实的伴侣和永恒的慰藉。

书籍具有不朽的本质，是为人类努力创造的最为持久的成果。寺庙会倒塌，神像会朽烂，而书却经久长存。对于伟大的思想来说，时间是无关紧要的。多年前初次闪现于作者脑海的伟大思想今日依然清新如故。时间唯一的作用是淘汰不好的作品，因为只有真正的佳作才能经世长存。

书籍介绍我们与最优秀的人为伍，使我们置身于历代伟人巨匠之间，如闻其声，如观其行，如见其人，同他们情感交融，悲喜与共，感同身受。我们觉得自己仿佛在作者所描绘的舞台上和他们一起粉墨登场。

即使在人世间，伟大杰出的人物也将永生。他们的精神被载入书册，传于四海。书是人生至今仍在聆听的智慧之声，永远充满着活力。

in this world. Embalmed in books, their spirits walk abroad. The book is a living voice. It is an intellect to which on still listens.

单词解析 Word Analysis

companionship [kəmˈpæniənʃɪp] *n.* 伙伴关系；友情

例 I depended on his companionship and on his judgment.
我信赖他的友情，也相信他的判断。

console [kənˈsəʊl] *v.* 安慰

例 Often they cry, and I have to play the role of a mother, consoling them.
经常他们一哭，我就要充当母亲的角色抚慰他们。

affinity [əˈfɪnəti] *n.* 密切关系；近似，类似

例 He has a close affinity with the landscape he knew when he was growing up.
他对这片从小就了解的土地有着一种归属感。
The two plots share certain obvious affinities.
这两个情节有某种明显的相似。

admiration [ˌædməˈreɪʃn] *n.* 钦佩，赞美；引人赞美的人或物

例 Meg's eyes widened in admiration.
梅格羡慕地睁大了双眼。

sympathize [ˈsɪmpəθaɪz] *v.* 同情，怜悯；赞同，支持

例 He would sympathize but he wouldn't understand.
他可能会表示同情，但不会理解。
Most of the people living there sympathized with the guerrillas.
住在那里的大多数人支持游击队。

urn [ɜːn] *n.* 壶；骨灰瓮

例 She put the big hot coffee urn on the table and plugged it in.
她将大咖啡壶放在桌子上，接上电源。

enshrine [ɪnˈʃraɪn] *v.* 放置或保存某物于；视……为神圣；珍藏；使……神圣不可侵犯

例 Southern farmers enshrine tombs on hillside terraces.
南方人把坟墓盖在山上。

The apartheid system which enshrined racism in law still existed.
以法律保护种族主义的种族隔离制度依旧存在。

treasure [ˈtreʒə(r)] *n.* 珍宝；不可多得的人才 *v.* 重视；珍惜；珍视

例 It was here, the buried treasure, she knew it was.
就在这里，那些埋藏在地下的财宝，她知道就在这里。

She treasures her memories of those joyous days.
她珍视那段快乐时光的记忆。

immortality [ˌɪmɔːˈtæləti] *n.* 不朽；不朽的声名（immoral 的名词形式）

例 No other people has been so obsessed with immortality as the Egyptian.
没有哪一个国家的人能像埃及人那样，喜欢追求不朽的东西。

The pharaohs were considered gods and therefore immortal.
法老们被视为神灵，且长生不死。

语法知识点 Grammar points

① **A man may usually be known by the books he reads as well as by the company he keeps.**

as well as 既……又……；除……之外（也）

例 Flowers are chosen for their scent as well as their look.
选花不仅要观其形还要闻其香。

② **It does not turn its back upon us in times of adversity or distress.**

turn one's back upon/on 转过身背向；抛弃；走开

例 One should never turn his back on his home country.
一个人永远也不能背弃自己的祖国。

③ **They are by far the most lasting products of human effort.**

by far 到目前为止，尤其（与比较级或最高级连用）

例 Their area of the park—near the pizza boxes—is by far the most dense.
公园里靠近比萨盒子的是他们的区域，是到目前为止最密集的。

④ **Time is of no account with great thoughts, which are as fresh today as when they first passed through their author's minds ages ago.**

be of no account 不重要的。与之比较 on account of "因为，由于"后是不适合加从句的。

例 He was granted special admission on account of his effort.
由于他自己的努力，他被破格录取。
On account of his more elevated position, the general had the enemy at vantage.
因为处于较高的位置，那位将军占了敌人的上风。

经典名句 Famous Classics

1. There is no development physically or intellectually without effort, and effort means work.
   没有努力，就不会有身体上或智力上的成长，而努力意味干活。

2. A dream doesn't become reality through magic, it takes sweat, determination, and hard work.
   梦想不是靠魔术来实现，而是靠汗水、决心和努力。

3. Suffering is the most powerful teacher in life.
   苦难是人生最伟大的老师。

4. Great hopes make great men.
   伟大的希望造就伟大的人物。

5. Man proposes, God disposes.
   谋事在人，成事在天。

24 College—A Transition Point in My Life
大学——我生命中的转折点

When I first entered college as a **freshman**, I was afraid that I was off by myself, away from my family for the first time. Here I was surrounded by people I did not know and who did not know me. I would have to make friends with them and perhaps also compete with them for grades in courses I would take. Were they smarter than I was? Could I keep up with them? Would they accept me?

I soon learned that my life was now up to me. I had to set a study program if I wanted to succeed in my courses. I had to **regulate** the time I spent studying and the time I spent **socializing**. I had to decide when to go to bed, when and what to eat, when and what to drink, and with whom to be friendly. These questions I had to answer for myself.

At first, life was a bit difficult. I made mistakes in how I used my time. I spent too much time making friends. I also made some mistakes in how to chose my first friends in college.

Shortly, however, I had my life under my control. I managed to go to class on time, do my first assignments and hand them in, and pass my first

当我以新生的身份进入大学时,我为自己担心,第一次离家那么远。在这儿,被我不认识也不认识我的人包围着。我不得不跟他们交朋友,也有可能要跟他们在我参加的课程上为学业竞争。他们比我聪明吗?我能赶上他们吗?他们会接受我吗?

很快我就认识到我的生活由我自己做主。我如果要在学业上取得成绩就必须为自己制定一个学习计划。我必须在学习的时间和社交的时间之间取得平衡。我不得不决定什么时候上床睡觉,什么时候吃东西和该吃什么,什么时间喝东西和该喝什么,还有,要对谁友善。这些都是该我自己去回答的了。

起初,生活有些辛苦了。我在怎样安排我的时间上犯了些错误。我花了太多时间去交朋友。我也在怎样在大学里交第一批朋友的问题上犯了错误。

当然,很快地,我重新掌控了自己的生活。我设法准时去教室上课,做好第一份作业然

137

exams with fairly good grades. In addition, I made a few friends with whom I felt comfortable and with whom I could share my fears. I set up a **routine** that was really my own—a routine that met my needs.

As a result, I began to look upon myself from a different **perspective**. I began to see myself as a person responsible for myself and responsible for my friends and family. It felt good to make my own decisions and see those decisions turn out to be wise ones. I guess that is all part of what people call "growing up."

What did life have in store for me? At that stage in my life, I really was not certain where I would **ultimately** go in life and what I would do with the years ahead of m. But I knew that I would be able to handle what was ahead because I had **successfully** jumped this important **hurdle** in my life: I had made the **transition** from a person dependent in my family for emotional support to a person who was responsible for myself.

后上交,以优异的成绩通过了第一次考试。此外,我交了几个朋友,跟他们待在一起我觉得很舒服,他们也可以分担我的担心。我建立了一个完完全全属于自己的时间表——一个可以满足我的需求的时间表。

然后,我开始用不同的视角来看待自己。我开始意识到自己要对自己负责,也要对我的朋友和家庭负责。我为能自己做决定,而且看到这些决定是明智的而感觉良好。我猜,这就是人们所说的"长大成人"。

生活为我准备了什么?在生命中的那个阶段,我实在不能确定最终我会去哪儿,接下来的日子我能干什么。但我知道我能主宰我的命运,因为我成功地跳过了这个生命中的重要障碍:我从一个需要从家庭汲取感情支持的人成为了一个能对自己负责任的人。

单词解析 Word Analysis

freshman ['freʃmən] *n.* (中学或大学的)一年级学生

例 It's important for the college freshman to keep his nose clean.
对大学新生而言洁身自好是很重要的。

College—A Transition Point in My Life
大学——我生命中的转折点

regulate ['reɡjuleɪt] *v.* 控制，管理

例 As we get older the temperature-regulating mechanisms in the body tend to become a little less efficient.
随着年龄的增长，人体体温调节机制的功能往往会有所弱化。

socializing ['səuʃəlaɪzɪŋ] *n.* 应酬；社交，是动词socialize的现在分词做名词的用法

例 However, too much socializing could lead to work piling up.
然而，过于爱交际则会导致工作干不完。

From the time you are born you have to be socialised into being a good father.
从出生的那一刻起，你就得学习融入群体，最后变成一个好父亲。

routine [ruːˈtiːn] *n.* 例行公事；惯例，惯常的程序

例 The players had to change their daily routine and lifestyle.
这些运动员不得不改变他们的日常生活习惯和方式。

The operator has to be able to carry out routine maintenance of the machine.
操作员必须能对机器进行日常维护。

perspective [pəˈspektɪv] *n.* 远景；前途（尤指受到某种思想、经验影响的）思考方法，态度

例 We may get a clear perspective of the people's happy lives.
我们知道人民对幸福生活的展望。

He says the death of his father 18 months ago has given him a new perspective on life.
他说18个月前父亲的去世让他对人生有了新的认识。

ultimately ['ʌltɪmətli] *adv.* 最后，最终

例 Ultimately, you'll have to make the decision yourself.
最终你还是得自己拿主意。

successfully [səkˈsesfəlɪ] *adv.* 顺利地；成功地

例 They successfully communicate their knowledge to others.
他们成功地把知识传授给他人。

hurdle ['hɜːdl] *n.* 障碍；困难

例 The weather will be the biggest hurdle so I have to be ready.
天气将会是最大的障碍，所以我必须要做好准备。

transition [træn'zɪʃn] *n.* 过渡；转变；变迁

例 He found the transition to boarding school excruciatingly painful.
他发现转到寄宿学校极其痛苦。

语法知识点 Grammar points

① I soon learned that my life was now up to me. I had to set a study program if I wanted to succeed in my courses.

up to 由……决定，由……负责

例 It's up to you whether we accept the present or not.
要不要这份礼物由你决定。

up to 有很多意思，比如多达；可与某事物相比，比得上；有某种能力的，能胜任的等。

例 I can take up to four people in my car.
我的车能载 4 个人。

As a doctor, he is not up to Mr. Smith.
作为一名医生，他不能与史密斯先生相比。

He's not up to the part of Othello.
他演不了奥赛罗这个角色。

② It felt good to make my own decisions and see those decisions turn out to be wise ones.

make one's decision 做决定

例 Some parents allow their children to make their own decisions.
有些家长允许孩子自己做决定。

turn out+to do 结果是；原来是

例 He said he was a doctor; but later he turned out to be a cheat.
他自称是个医生，结果证明他是个骗子。

③ What did life have in store for me?

College—A Transition Point in My Life
大学——我生命中的转折点

in store 将要发生，就要出现

> There are better days in store for you.
> 更好的日子在等着你。

经典名句 Famous Classics

1. Dishonesty is ultimately self-defeating.
   弄虚作假最终会自食其果。

2. Narrowly self-interested behaviour is ultimately self-defeating.
   狭隘自私的行为最终会自拆台脚。

3. Youth is the time to go flashing from one end of the world to the other both in mind and body; to try the manners of different nations; to hear the chimes at midnight; to see sunrise in town and country; to be converted at a revival; to circumnavigate the metaphysics, write halting verses, run a mile to see a fire, and wait all day long in the theatre to applaud *Hernani*.
   年轻的时候，就应该跑遍世界去展示自己的心灵与身体；去体验不同国度的生活；在午夜时聆听钟声敲响；在城镇乡村欣赏日出的景色；在训道时受到感化；看遍形而上学的著作，创作一些不完美的诗歌，跑很远的路去看一场焰火，在剧院里等上一天，只为了为《欧那尼》鼓掌欢呼。

4. Nothing ever becomes real till it is experienced—Even a Proverb is no proverb to you till your Life has illustrated it.
   没有经历过的事不是真实的——即使是格言，在你的人生验证了它之前，它对你来说也不是格言。

5. Do not look back. And do not dream about the future, either. It will neither give you back the past, nor satisfy your other daydreams. Your duty, your reward—your destiny—are here and now.
   不要总是回顾过去，也不要总是梦想未来。这样做既不会让你回到过去，也不会实现你的美梦。你的责任，你的回报——你的命运——就在当下。

6. When I think of all the books I have read, and of the wise words I have heard spoken, and of the anxiety I have given to parents and grandparents, and of the hopes that I have had, all life weighed in the scales of my own life seems to me preparation for something that never happens.
当我回顾我曾经读过的书，曾经听过的箴言警句，曾经给长辈带来的烦恼，曾经有过的希冀，我的整个生命衡量起来，仿佛是在为一些从未发生的事情做准备。

7. We combat obstacles in order to get repose, and, when got, the repose is insupportable.
我们为了得到安宁而去战胜阻碍，当我们终于成功时，却不堪忍受这种安宁。

8. From the satisfaction of desire there may arise, accompanying joy and as it were sheltering behind it, something not unlike despair.
当欲望被满足时，伴随着快乐，同时躲在它身后而来的，是一种很像是绝望的东西。

9. Most people get a fair amount of fun out of their lives, but on balance life is suffering, and only the very young or the very foolish imagine otherwise.
大多数人一生中有许多快乐，但综合来说人生是痛苦的，只有年轻人和愚蠢之人才不这样想。

10. Time lost is time when we have not lived a full human life, time unenriched by experience, creative endeavor, enjoyment, and suffering.
我们浪费的时间就是我们没有充实的生活的时间，没有亲身体验，没有去冒险、享受和感受痛苦的时间。

11. One of the most obvious facts about grown-ups, to a child, is that they have forgotten what it is like to be a child.
对孩子们来说，大人们最明显的特点就是他们已经忘了怎么去当一个孩子。

25 Weakness or Strength
弱点还是强项

Sometimes our biggest weakness can become your biggest strength. Take, for example, the story of one 10-year-old boy who decided to study **judo despite** the fact that he had lost his left arm in a **devastating** car accident.

The boy began lesson with an old Japanese judo master. The boy was done well, so he couldn't understand why, after three months of training, the master had taught him only one move.

"**Sensei**," the boy finally said, "shouldn't I be learning more moves?"

"This is the only move you know, but this is the only move you'll ever need to know," the sensei replied.

Not quite understanding, but believing in his teacher, the boy kept training.

Several months later, the master took the boy to his first **tournament**.

To his surprise, the boy easily won his first two matches. The third match proved to be more difficult, but after some time, his opponent became impatient and charged; the boy **deftly** used his one move to win the match. Still amazed by his success, the boy

有的时候，你的弱项可以变成你的强项。给你讲一个10岁男孩的故事做例子。这个男孩在一次惨烈的车祸中失去了左臂，但他仍然决定学习柔道。

男孩师从一位年长的日本柔道大师。孩子练得很好，但他不明白为什么师傅在三个月的训练中，始终只让他重复同一个动作。

"师傅，"男孩终于忍不住问道，"我是不是可以学点儿别的动作了？"

师傅回答说："这是你唯一知道的动作，但也是你唯一需要知道的动作。"

男孩虽然不理解，但他非常信任自己的师傅，于是继续练着。

几个月后，师傅带这个男孩子去参加他的第一次比赛。

令这个男孩不可思议的是，他轻易赢了头两场比赛。第三场比赛似乎更难，但他的对手在比赛中开始失去耐心，向他冲过来，而这个孩子立即用他学过的唯一一招击败了对手。就这样稀里糊涂地，他进

was now in the finals. This time, his opponent was bigger, stronger, and more experienced. For a while, the boy appeared to be overmatched. Concerned that the boy might get hurt, the referee called a time-out. He was about to stop the match when the master **intervened**.

"No," his master insisted, "let him continue."

Soon after the match resumed, his opponent made a **critical** mistake: he dropped his guard. **Instantly**, the boy used his move to pin him. The boy had won the match and the tournament. He was the champion.

On the way home, the boy and his master reviewed every move in each and every match. Then the boy summoned the courage to ask what was really in his min.

"Master, how did I win the tournament with only one move?"

"You won for two reasons," the master answered, "First, you've almost mastered one of the most difficult throws in all of judo. Second, the only known defense for that move is for your **opponent** to grab your left arm."

The boy's biggest weakness had become his biggest strength.

入了决赛。这一次，他的对手更壮、更强，也更有经验。有那么一阵，男孩似乎抵挡不住了。考虑到男孩可能会受伤，裁判叫了暂停。他正准备停止比赛的时候，男孩的师傅阻止了他。

"不能停，"他说，"让他继续比。"

比赛继续进行之后不久，男孩的对手就犯了一个致命的错误：防漏（柔道术语）。男孩迅速用他那唯一的一招绊倒了对手，赢了这场比赛，并最终取得了冠军。

回家的路上，当男孩和他师傅重温着每一场比赛里的每一个动作时，他鼓起勇气道出了心中的困惑。

"师傅，我怎么会用一个动作就赢得了所有的比赛呢？"

"你获胜有两个原因，"师傅回答道，"第一，你已经基本掌握了柔道当中最难学的一个动作。第二，要对付这个动作，你的对手唯一可以做的就是去抓你的左臂。"

就这样，男孩的最大弱点变成了他的最强项。

Weakness or Strength
弱点还是强项 25

单词解析 Word Analysis

judo [ˈdʒuːdəʊ] *n.* （日）柔道

例 The judo is a kind of fighting sport.
柔道是一种对抗性体育活动。

despite [dɪˈspaɪt] *prep.* 尽管，虽然

例 Despite a thorough investigation, no trace of Dr Southwell has been found.
尽管进行了彻底的调查，还是没有发现索思韦尔博士的任何踪迹。

devastating [ˈdevəsteɪtɪŋ] *adj.* 毁灭性的；全然的

例 Affairs do have a devastating effect on marriages.
婚外情确实会对婚姻造成毁灭性的影响。

sensei [senˈsiː] *n.* 老师

例 At this rate, there's no way I can beat Kakashi sensei.
以这种程度，我没办法打败卡卡西老师。

tournament [ˈtʊənəmənt] *n.* 比赛；锦标赛，联赛

例 The tournament is open to both amateurs and professionals.
这次锦标赛业余选手和职业选手均可参加。

deftly [ˈdeftlɪ] *adv.* 灵巧地；熟练地；敏捷地（deft是形容词形式）

例 With a deft flick of his foot, Mr. Worth tripped one of the raiders up.
沃思先生机敏地把脚一伸，把其中一个袭击者给绊倒了。
It was wonderful to watch her fingers moving deftly and unerringly.
观看她的手指灵巧而又准确无误地移动是一件美事。

intervene [ˌɪntəˈviːn] *v.* 干涉，干预

例 The situation calmed down when police intervened.
警方干预后，局势平息下来。

critical [ˈkrɪtɪkl] *adj.* 决定性的；评论的；批评的；爱挑剔的

例 Their chief negotiator turned his critical eye on the United States.
他们的首席谈判代表以批判的眼光看美国。

The incident happened at a critical point in the campaign.
该事件发生在竞选活动的关键时期。

instantly [ˈɪnstəntli] *adv.* 立刻，立即

例 You are protected instantly if a thief misuses your credit card.
如果小偷盗用你的信用卡，你的卡会立即受到保护。

opponent [əˈpəʊnənt] *n.* 对手；敌手；反对者

例 He's the best opponent I've come across this season, a great player.
他是我本赛季遇到的最出色的对手，一位了不起的运动员。

He became an outspoken opponent of the old Soviet system.
他成为旧的苏联体制直言不讳的抨击者。

语法知识点 *Grammar points*

① **Take, for example, the story of one 10-year-old boy who decided to study judo despite the fact that he had lost his left arm in a devastating car accident.**

该句中包括一个由who引导的定语从句，先行词为boy，和一个同位语从句the fact that，其中that不可省。

② **Not quite understanding, but believing in his teacher, the boy kept training.**

believe in sb. 信任某人

例 We believe in him, who is always true to his word.
我们信任他，他总是说话算话的。

keep doing 一直做

例 Keep doing your homework so you don't get behind in school.
坚持写你们的家庭作业，这样你们就不会在学习上掉队。

③ **Concerned that the boy might get hurt, the referee called a time-out.**

该句中的concerned为分词形容词做状语。

例 Encouraged by the speech, the young people made up their minds to take up the struggle.

Weakness or Strength
弱点还是强项 25

受到了演讲的鼓舞，年轻人决定从事斗争。

get hurt 受伤

例 Compassion includes ourselves too—we can't let ourselves get hurt in the process.
怜悯同样包括我们自己——我们不能让自己在这个过程中受伤。

④ **On the way home, the boy and his master reviewed every move in each and every match. Then the boy summoned the courage to ask what was really in his min.**

on one's way to 在……路上，后面可以加地点，表示"去……的路上"。

例 She was on her way to the supermarket when she was knocked down by a car.
她在去超市的路上被车撞倒了。

经典名句 Famous Classics

1. Disease, enemy, and debt—these three must be cut off as soon as they begin to grow.
   疾病、敌人和债务，这三样事物一露苗头便应除之。

2. What some call health, if purchased by perpetual anxiety about diet, isn't much better than tedious disease.
   通过长期控制饮食而得来的所谓健康，并不比某种慢性疾病好到哪里去。

3. A wise man should consider that health is the greatest of human blessings, and learn how by his own thought to derive benefit from his illnesses.
   有智慧的人应该把健康当作最珍贵的恩赐，并且学习怎样从他的疾病中吸取经验。

4. A vigorous five-mile walk will do more good for and unhappy but otherwise healthy adult than all the medicine and psychology in the world.
   快速地走上五英里，对一个情绪低落但是身体健康的人来说，比任何药物与心理治疗都有用。

147

5. Be careful about reading health books. You may die of a misprint.
   阅读健康方面的书籍时要小心，你会因为印刷错误而送了性命的。

6. To live long is almost everyone's wish, but to live well is the ambition of a few.
   人人皆想活得长，鲜少有人想要活得好。

7. Health does not consist with intemperance.
   健康和放纵，彼此不相容。

8. The sick are the greatest threat to the healthy. Not from the strongest but from the weakest does harm come to the strong.
   染上疾病的人对健康的人是最大的威胁。强者往往是被最弱小，而非最强大的人们伤害。

9. The wretcheder one is, the more one smokes; and the more one smokes, the wretcheder one gets —a vicious circle!
   一个人越是烦恼，就越要抽烟；而他抽得越多，就越烦恼——这是恶性循环！

10. The discovery of a new dish does more for human happiness than the discovery of a star.
    新食谱的发明比新星体的发现更让人们开心。

读书笔记

26 Feed Your Mind
别让你的脑子挨饿

Since the pre historic times man has had an **urge** to satisfy his needs. Be it hunger, shelter or search for a mate, he has always **manipulated** the circumstances to the best of his advantages. Probably this might be the reason why we human are the most developed of all living species on the earth and probably also in the universe. As we climbed the steps of **evolution** with giant leaps, we somehow left behind common sense and logical thinking we forgot that we have stopped thinking ahead of times.

If you are hungry, what do you do? Grab a piece of your favorite meal and stay quiet after that? Just like your **stomach**, even your mind is hungry. But it never lets you know, because you keep it busy thinking about your dream lover favorite star and many such **absurd** things. So it silently began to **heed** to your needs and never let itself grow. When mind **looses** its freedom to grow, creativity gets a full stop. This might be the reason why we all sometimes think "What happens next?", "Why can t I think?", "Why am I always given the difficult problems?" Well, this is

自史前时代起，人类就已有满足自己需求的强烈欲望。无论是饥饿、避难或寻觅配偶，人类总是操纵着环境使其达到最利于自己的状态。这或许解答了为什么人类是地球上甚至是宇宙中最高级的现存物种。然而在进化的阶梯上取得巨大飞跃之时，我们却不知何故将一些常识和逻辑思维抛诸脑后了——我们忘记了自己已经停止了超前思维。

如果你饿了，你会怎么做？抓起你最喜爱的美食饱餐一顿，然后静静地待在那里？而你的大脑也像你的胃，是会感到饥饿的，但它却从不让你知道，因为你让它一直想着你的梦中情人、你最喜爱的明星和许多诸如此类的荒唐事。因此它只是默默地留意着你的需要却从不让自己成长。当思维恣意成长时，创造力就戛然而止。这也许就是为什么我们有时会想下一步该如何？为什么我想不到？为什么我总是碰到难题的原因吧。这也是我们的大脑总在考虑那些毫无价值的

149

the **aftermath** of our own **karma** of using our brain for thinking of not so worthy things.

Hunger of the mind can be actually **satiated** through **extensive** reading. Now why reading and not watching TV? Because reading has been the most educative tool used by us right from the childhood. Just like that to develop other aspects of our life, we have to take help of reading. You have **innumerable** number of books in this world which will answer all your "How to" questions. Once you read a book, you just don't run your eyes through the lines but even your mind **decodes** it and explains it to you. The interesting part of the book is stored in your mind as a seed. Now this seed is **unknowingly** used by you in your future to develop new ideas. The same seed if used many times can help you link and relate a lot of things of which you would have never thought of in your wildest dreams. This is nothing but creativity. More the number of books you read your mind will open up like never before.

事情产生的后果。

事实上，思维的饥荒可以通过广泛的阅读来满足。为什么是阅读而不是选择看电视呢？因为自孩提时代起，读书就已经是最具教育性的工具了。正如人生发展的其他方面一样，我们不得不求助于阅读。世界上有无数书籍可以回答你如何做的问题。读书时不仅要用眼睛浏览文字，还要用脑去解读、诠释。书中有趣的部分就会像种子一样贮存在你的脑海里。将来你会不自觉地运用这粒种子引发新的想法。多次运用这粒种子将有助于你把许多事情联系起来，即使你做梦都想不到这些！这不是别的，就是创造力！你读的书越多，你的心智就会前所未有地开阔。

单词解析 Word Analysis

urge [ɜːdʒ] *n.* 冲动 *v.* 催促；推进

例 He slipped his arm around her waist and urged her away from the window.

Feed Your Mind 26
别让你的脑子挨饿

他揽住她的腰，拉着她离开了窗边。
He had an urge to open a shop of his own.
他很想自己开一家店。

manipulate [mə'nɪpjuleɪt] *v.* 摆布，操纵，控制（他人）

例 He is a very difficult character. He manipulates people.
他是个极难对付的角色，总是把人玩弄于股掌之间。

evolution [ˌiːvə'luːʃn] *n.* 演变；进化；发展

例 A cultural and social evolution now becomes rapid.
现在文化和社会发展很快。

stomach ['stʌmək] *adj.* 胃；胃口；腹部

例 My stomach is completely full.
我完全吃饱了。

absurd [əb'sɜːd] *a.* 荒谬的；可笑的

例 I've known clients of mine go to absurd lengths, just to avoid paying me a few pounds.
我知道我的一些客户就为了少付我几英镑，可谓无所不用其极。

heed [hiːd] *v.* 注意，留心

例 He pays too much heed these days to my nephew Tom, and Tom is no great thinker.
他最近过分重视我侄子汤姆的话了，而汤姆根本不是什么伟大的思想家。

loose [luːs] *v.* 释放；开船；放枪 *adj.* 松动的；未固定牢的

例 T If a tooth feels very loose, your dentist may recommend that it's taken out.
如果有一颗牙齿很松，牙医可能会建议你把它拔掉。
He gave a grunt and loosed his grip on the rifle.
他闷哼了一声，松开了握着来复枪的手。

aftermath ['ɑːftəmæθ] *n.* 后果；余波

例 In the aftermath of the hurricane, many people's homes were destroyed.
飓风的后果是许多人的房屋被毁。

我的人生美文：那些随风飘逝的日子

karma ['kɑːmə] *n.* 因果报应，因缘
例 But what happens when karma turns right around and bites you.
但如果当报应回过头来咬你。

satiated ['seɪʃɪeɪtɪd] *adj.* 对……厌倦的；充分满足的；生腻的
例 The dinner was enough to satiate the gourmets.
晚餐足以让这些美食家们大饱口福。

extensive [ɪk'stensɪv] *adj.* 广泛的；广阔的；大量的
例 The blast caused extensive damage, shattering the ground-floor windows.
爆炸造成了巨大的破坏，震碎了一楼的窗户。
The resort is surrounded by extensive national and regional parklands.
那个度假胜地被广阔的国家和地区绿地所环绕。

innumerable [ɪ'njuːmərəbl] *adj.* 无数的，数不清的
例 He has invented innumerable excuses, told endless lies.
他编造了数不清的借口和谎话。

decode [ˌdiː'kəʊd] *v.* 译码，解码
例 All he had to do was decode it and pass it over.
他需要做的就是将它破译然后转给他人。

unknowingly [ʌn'nəʊɪŋlɪ] *adv.* 不知不觉地
例 All things are this way, comes and goes may also unknowingly.
一切事物都是这样，来得快，去得也一样不知不觉。

语法知识点 Grammar points

① **Be it hunger, shelter or search for a mate, he has always manipulated the circumstances to the best of his advantages.**

to the best of 尽最大努力
例 You can be part of this change by doing your job to the best of your ability.
你能够通过在工作中发挥自己最大的才能来参与这一改变。

To the best of my knowledge we have the lowest turnover in the tech industry.

据我所知，我们公司的人员流动率在高科技行业内是最低的。

② **This might be the reason why we all sometimes think "What happens next?""Why can't I think?" "Why am I always given the difficult problems?"**

the reason why... 发生……的原因是……

例 Tell me the reason why he did not come.
告诉我他没来的原因。

③ **Just like that to develop other aspects of our life, we have to take help of reading.**

take help of 求助于……

例 Never take the help of brokers or traders.
从未采取经纪人或交易商的帮助。

just like 正如，就好像

例 Men go through a change of life emotionally just like women.
男人和女人一样，也要在情绪上经历更年期。

④ **The same seed if used many times, can help you link and relate a lot of things, of which you would have never thought of in your wildest dreams!**

本句话为非限制性定语从句，引导词是of which，注意这里的which不可以换成that，因为前面有介词of，而且that不可以引导非限制性定语从句。

例 She may be late, in which case we ought to wait for her.
她可能晚到，那样我们就要等等她。

经典名句 Famous Classics

1. They're just like eggs hurled against stone; they're heading for their doom.
鸡蛋怎能碰得过石头，还不是自寻死路。

2. Look to your health; and if you have it, praise God, and value it

next to a good conscience; for health is the second blessing that we mortals are capable of; a blessing that money cannot buy.
留意你的健康；如果你拥有健康，那么赞美上帝，并且珍视它，健康仅次于一个明智的头脑；健康是我们凡人能够得到的第二好的恩赐，这是金钱买不到的。

3. Why waste money on psychotherapy when you can listen to the B Minor Mass?
何必把钱浪费在心理治疗上呢，去听B小调弥撒吧。

4. 1 billion people in the world are chronically hungry. 1 billion people are overweight.
世界上有十亿人在挨饿，也有十亿人体重超标。

5. A torn jacket is soon mended; but hard words bruise the heart of a child.
被扯坏的衣服很容易修补，而伤人的话语会伤害孩子的心灵。

6. You are worried about seeing him spend his early years in doing nothing. What! Is it nothing to be happy? Nothing to skip, play, and run around all day long? Never in his life will he be so busy again.
你担心他（孩子们）会把童年浪费掉吗？你说什么？感到快乐是浪费时间吗？一整天都蹦跳着玩耍、奔跑是浪费时间吗？他这一生都不会再比这更忙了。

7. In all our efforts to provide "advantages" we have actually produced the busiest, most competitive, highly pressured, and over-organized generation of youngsters in our history—and possibly the unhappiest.
我们在竭力为孩子们创造"优势"的时候，我们实际上创造出了一群最忙碌、最有竞争意识、最有压力同时过于自律的一代年轻人，他们也很有可能是最不开心的一群人。

8. The United States in the 1980's may be the first society in history in which children are distinctly worse off than adults.
20世纪80年代的美国也许是历史上头一次让孩子们过着比成年人更劳苦的生活。

Feed Your Mind
别让你的脑子挨饿

9. The more people have studied different methods of bringing up children the more they have come to the conclusion that what good mother and fathers instinctively feel like doing for their babies is the best after all.
越多人去研究教育之道，就会有越多人发现，父母的直觉往往是最正确的。

10. Grown-ups never understand anything for themselves, and it is tiresome for children to be always and forever explaining things to them.
大人们总是什么都不明白，孩子们总要不厌其烦地解释给他们听。

读书笔记

27 Run Out of the Rainy Season of Your Life
跑出人生的雨季

My life suffered a lot in a summer five years ago. My father died of an accident resulted from drinking, leaving my **emaciated** mother and two younger brothers alone. At that time, I was in a senior high school. After my father's **funeral**, the whole family was in a worse condition than ever. As the eldest son, I had no choice but to quit school and work in a factory.

　Life went on without any wonder. I dare not to ask for more, just hoping to bring up two younger brothers. However, that's not an easy thing, for I can't afford their **tuition** even if I work from day to night without stopping, and much worse, I must take my sick mother into account. The present **misery** made me want to have another try, but it seems **impractical**, for I can't lose this job any more.

　A thread of hope sparkled in those gloomy days suddenly. It was a rainy dusk when I put myself in the rain and walked in the street.

　Suddenly the rain stopped! To my **bewilderment**, I raised my head, and found that "the sky" was in fact a dark

5年前的夏天，我的人生痛苦不堪。父亲因酗酒死于一场事故，撇下了我瘦弱的母亲和两个弟弟。那时，我正上高中。父亲葬礼后，全家人比以前的状态更加糟糕。作为长子，我别无选择，只好退学，到一家工厂打工。

日子就这样平淡无奇地过着。我不敢再有更多的奢求，只希望把两个弟弟抚养成人。然而，那不是轻而易举的事儿。因为即使我每天从早到晚不停工作，也难以支付他们的学费，更何况我必须考虑多病的母亲。眼前的困境使我想再努力一次，但又好像不切实际，因为我不能再丢掉这份工作。

一线希望突然照亮了那些阴暗的日子。那是一个雨天的黄昏，我置身雨中，走在街上。

雨突然停了，我感到迷惑，就抬起头，发现"天空"其实是一顶深蓝色的伞。随后，我听到一个深沉的声音，"没有伞，为什么不跑？"一位拄着拐杖的独腿中年人对我说，"如果跑，你就不会被淋

Run Out of the Rainy Season of Your Life
跑出人生的雨季

blue umbrella. Then I heard a deep voice. "Why not running without an umbrella?" a **middle-aged** man with one leg on crutch said to me, "If you run, you would get less **drenched**." I shook my head, but after a second I thought: Right, why not running without an umbrella? His words shocked me deeply. Without my father's protection, could I only be a slave to the fate, and my dream in childhood only an **illusion**?

While walking together in the rain, I knew that he was a **promoter** from the city, and he received an order and paid much time on it. Facing this guy, I had no **sympathy** but admiration. I took the umbrella from his right hand and he told me that he once had dreamed of being a policeman, but an accident ruined his dream. Though his present work was demanding and did not suit for his leg, every outing was a wonderful start to him. He was glad that he didn't lose heart and still "ran" on the road of life…

It seems that everything is destined but not always. **Enlightened** by the man's remarks, I went to a city in the south and became an assurance representative. After two years' "running", I got somewhere and my family turned better gradually. I came back to my senior high school for the dream in my childhood. The year before last summer, I eventually

得湿透。"我摇摇头，却转念又一想：没有伞，为什么不跑呢？他的话普通却深深地震撼了我。没有了父亲的保护，我就只能做命运的奴隶，童年的梦想就只能是幻想吗？

雨中同行时，我知道了他是城里来的推销员，他接到了一份订单，为此花费了很多时间。面对这个人，我没有怜悯，只有钦佩。我默默地从他的右手里接过伞。他告诉我说他曾想做一名警察，但一次意外事故毁灭了他的梦想。尽管现在的工作非常苛刻，不适合他这腿，但每次出门对他来说都是一个奇妙的开始。他很高兴自己没有丧失勇气，仍然"跑"在人生的道路上……

一切都似乎是命中注定，但又不总是那样。那个人的话让我深受启发，我去了南方的一个城市，成了一名保险代理人。通过两年的"奔跑"，我取得了一些业绩，家境也渐渐好转。因为童年的梦想，我又回到了高中。前年夏天，我终于考上了大学。

生活就是这样：当你处在人生的雨季时，如果你无法尽快找到防止雨淋的方法，就要被雨水淋透，但如果你决定摆脱，你会发现，雨季并非像你

succeeded in my entrance to university.

　　Life is like this: When you are in rainy days in your life, if you couldn't find a way to prevent you from being drenched earlier, you would have been overwhelmed by it, but if you decided to get rid of it, you'll discover that the rainy days last not so long as you imagined.

　　Everything is so simple: To run without an umbrella! When you run out of the rainy season of your life, there will be bright sky ahead of you.

原来想的那样长。

　　一切都是那么简单：没有伞，就跑！跑出人生的雨季，你前面就会是一片晴朗的天空。

单词解析 Word Analysis

emaciated [ɪˈmeɪʃɪeɪtɪd] *adj.* 瘦弱的，憔悴的，动词的过去分词做形容词的用法

例 The animals had lost weight noticeably, becoming lean, almost emaciated.
那些动物体重明显下降，瘦多了，简直是憔悴不堪。

funeral [ˈfjuːnərəl] *n.* 葬礼，丧礼；〈比喻〉不愉快的事

例 His funeral will be on Thursday at Blackburn Cathedral.
他的葬礼将于星期四在布莱克本大教堂举行。

tuition [tjuˈɪʃn] *n.* 学费

例 Angela's $7, 000 tuition at University this year will be paid for with scholarships.
安杰拉将用奖学金支付今年7,000美元的大学学费。

misery [ˈmɪzəri] *n.* 痛苦；不幸；穷困；悲惨的境遇

例 All that money brought nothing but sadness and misery and tragedy.
那笔钱带来的只有伤心、痛苦和悲剧。

Run Out of the Rainy Season of Your Life 27
跑出人生的雨季

impractical [ɪmˈpræktɪkl] *adj.* 不切实际的；无用的

例 It became impractical to make a business trip by ocean liner.
乘坐远洋班轮进行商务旅行变得不合时宜了。

bewilderment [bɪˈwɪldəmənt] *n.* 迷惘，困惑，迷乱

例 He shook his head in bewilderment.
他困惑地摇了摇头。

middle-aged [ˈmɪdl eɪdʒd] *adj.* 中年的；具有中年人特点的，保守的，过时的

例 His sisters are grown up and his parents are middle-aged.
他的姐妹们都已成人，而他的父母亲也人到中年。
Her novels are middle-aged and boring.
她的小说刻板乏味。

drenched [drentʃd] *adj.* 湿透的；充满的

例 They were getting drenched by icy water.
他们被冰冷的水浇透了。

illusion [ɪˈluːʒn] *n.* 错觉，幻想；假象

例 No one really has any illusions about winning the war.
没有人幻想能赢得这场战争。

promoter [prəˈməʊtə(r)] *n.* 发起人；促进者

例 She became a leading promoter of European integration.
她成为欧洲一体化的主要支持者。

sympathy [ˈsɪmpəθi] *n.* 同情，同情心

例 I have had very little help from doctors and no sympathy whatsoever.
我从医生那里没有得到什么帮助，也未获得丝毫同情。

enlightened [ɪnˈlaɪtn] *v.* 启发，启蒙

例 If you know what is wrong with her, please enlighten me.
如果你知道她出什么问题了，请告诉我。

159

语法知识点 *Grammar points*

① **My father died of an accident resulted from drinking, leaving my emaciated mother and two younger brothers alone.**

die of 死于……，通常情况下死因存在于人体之上或之内（主要指疾病、衰老等自身的原因），若死因是环境影响到体内，即两方面共有的原因，则可用of, from均可。die from指死因不是存在人体之内或之上，而是由环境造成的（主要指事故等方面的外部原因）。

例 His grandfather died of liver cancer in 1992.
　　他的祖父1992年死于肝癌。

　　The old man died from a car accident last year.
　　老人去年死于车祸。

result from产生于……，由……引起。句中resulted from是现在分词短语做后置定语，修饰accident。

例 The first solution, strictly, does not result from an analysis.
　　严格地说第一组解并不是由分析得出的结果。

② **I dare not to ask for more, just hoping to bring up two younger brothers.**

bring up 在文中意为"养育，抚养"。

例 His grandmother and his father brought him up.
　　是他的祖母和父亲把他养大的。

除此以外，还有"提出""呕出"等意。

例 It's hard for the baby to bring up wind.
　　婴儿不容易打出嗝来。

　　Instead of staying in the here and now, you bring up similar instances from the past.
　　你没有紧扣眼前所发生的事，而是只提出了一些过去的类似事例。

③ **I took the umbrella from his right hand and he told me that he once had dreamed of being a policeman, but an accident ruined his dream.**

dream of 渴望，向往，考虑

例 He has dreamt of wealth and happiness.
　　他渴望富有和幸福。

Run Out of the Rainy Season of Your Life
跑出人生的雨季 **27**

I dream of becoming a teacher.
我一心想当个教师。

相似的词组还有dream about，表示"梦见"。

例 I sometimes dream about my parents.
我有时梦见我的父母。

④ When you run out of the rainy season of your life, there will be bright sky ahead of you.

run out of 从……跑出；耗尽

例 The aircraft will run out of fuel in another hour.
飞机再过一小时燃料就将用完。

经典名句 Famous Classics

1. You make the failure complete when you stop trying.
   当你停止尝试的时候，你就完全失败了。

2. Difficult circumstances serve as a textbook of life for people.
   困难坎坷是人们的生活教科书。

3. When all else is lost the future still remains.
   就算失去了一切，也还有未来。

读书笔记

28 Eating the Cookie
生活的真谛

One of my patients, a successful businessman, tells me that before his cancer he would become **depressed** unless things went a certain way. Happiness was "having the cookie". If you had the cookie, things were good. If you didn't have the cookie, life wasn't worth a **damn**. **Unfortunately**, the cookie kept changing. Some of the time it was money, sometimes power, sometimes sex. At other times, it was the new car, the biggest **contract**, the most **prestigious** address. A year and a half after his **diagnosis** of **prostate** cancer he sits shaking his head **ruefully**. "It's like I stopped learning how to live after I was a kid. When I give my son a cookie, he is happy. If I take the cookie away or it breaks, he is unhappy. But he is two and a half and I am forty-three. It's taken me this long to understand that the cookie will never make me happy for long. The minute you have the cookie it starts to **crumble** or you start to worry about it crumbling or about someone trying to take it away from you. You know, you have to give up a lot of things to take care of the

我有一位病人，他是一个成功的商人，他告诉我，在他患癌症之前，凡事如果没有确定下来他就忧心忡忡。对他而言，幸福是"拥有小甜饼"。如果你拥有了小甜饼，一切都一帆风顺。如果你没有小甜饼，生活就一文不值。不幸的是，小甜饼总是不断变换着，有时是金钱，有时是权力，有时是欲望。在其他时候，它是一辆新车、一份数额最大的合同，或者一个享有声望的通讯地址。在他被诊断出患有前列腺癌的一年半之后，他坐在那里，悲天悯人地摇着头，说："长大以后，我好像就不知道怎样生活了。当我给我儿子一个小甜饼时，他心花怒放。如果我拿走甜饼或者是小甜饼碎了，他就闷闷不乐。不同的是，他只有两岁半，而我已经43岁了。我花了这么长的时间才明白小甜饼并不能使我长久感到幸福。从你拥有小甜饼的那一刻，它就开始破碎，或者你就开始担心它会破碎，抑或你开始担心别人拿走它。为了守护你的小甜饼，为了防止它破碎或者确定

Eating the Cookie
生活的真谛 28

cookie, to keep it from crumbling and be sure that no one takes it away from you. You may not even get a chance to eat it because you are so busy just trying not to lose it. Having the cookie is not what life is about."

My patient laughs and says cancer has changed him. For the first time he is happy, no matter if his business is doing well or not, no matter if he wins or loses at golf. Two years ago, cancer asked me, "Okay, What's important? What is really important?" Well, life is important. Life, anyway, you can have it, life with the cookie, life without the cookie. Happiness does not have anything to do with the cookie; it has to do with being alive. Before, who made the time? He pauses **thoughtfully**. "Damn, I guess life is the cookie."

别人不会从你手中夺走它,你不得不放弃许多东西。你忙于不让自己失去它,甚至没有时间享受它。拥有小甜饼并不是生活的全部内容。"

我的病人笑着说癌症已经改变了他。不论他的生意是否一帆风顺,不论他在打高尔夫球时是输是赢,他有生以来第一次感到幸福。两年前,癌症问我"什么重要?什么才真正重要?"对,生命重要。生命,无论如何你拥有生命。有小甜饼也罢,没有小甜饼也罢,幸福与小甜饼并非息息相关,而是与生命的存在有关。可是,时光一去不复返,谁又能让时光倒流呢?他停顿了一下,若有所思,说:"该死,我觉得生命就是那块小甜饼。"

单词解析 Word Analysis

depressed [dɪ'prest] *adj.* 沮丧的;萧条的

> She's been very depressed and upset about this whole situation.
> 她对整个情形感到极其沮丧和不快。
> The construction industry is no longer as depressed as it was.
> 建筑业不再像以往那样萧条了。

damn [dæm] *n.* 一点也不,丝毫

> There's not a damn thing you can do about it now.
> 现在你对此做什么都完全无济于事。

163

unfortunately [ʌnˈfɔːtʃənətli] *adv.* 不幸地，遗憾地；可惜地

例 Unfortunately, my time is limited.
可惜的是，我的时间有限。
Unfortunately, there is little prospect of seeing these big questions answered.
不幸的是，几乎不可能看到这些重大问题得到回复。

contract [ˈkɒntrækt] *n.* 合同，契约

例 He was given a seven-year contract with an annual salary of $150,000.
他签下了一份为期7年的合同，年薪为15万美元。

prestigious [preˈstɪdʒəs] *adj.* 有威望的，受尊敬的

例 It's one of the best equipped and most prestigious schools in the country.
这是国内设备最先进、最有威望的学校之一。

diagnosis [ˌdaɪəgˈnəʊsɪs] *n.* 诊断，诊断结果

例 I need to have a second test to confirm the diagnosis.
我需要再进行一次检查以确诊。

prostate [ˈprɒsteɪt] *n.* 前列腺

例 Poor dietary habits are strongly linked to prostate dysfunction as well.
不良的饮食习惯也是导致前列腺功能障碍的重大因素。

ruefully [ˈruːfəli] *adv.* 悲伤地，可怜地（形容词rueful）

例 He shook his head and gave me a rueful smile.
他摇了摇头，遗憾地对我笑了笑。

crumble [ˈkrʌmbl] *v.* 碎裂，破碎

例 Roughly crumble the cheese into a bowl.
把干酪大致弄碎，装入一只碗内。

thoughtfully [ˈθɔːtfəli] *adv.* 沉思地；深虑地（形容词thoughtful）

例 She rubbed her chin thoughtfully.
她若有所思地抚摸着下巴。

Eating the Cookie 生活的真谛 28

Thank you. That's very thoughtful of you.
谢谢你，你想的真周到。

语法知识点 Grammar points

① **If you had the cookie, things were good. If you didn't have the cookie, life wasn't worth a damn.**

worth a damn 值得，这是worth后接名词的用法，worth是一个只能做表语的形容词，意思是"值得……""有……价值的"
be worth sth. 值……

例 These books might be worth £80 or £90 or more to a collector.
这些书对收藏家而言可能值八九十英镑或更多。

worth后面如果跟动词，必须要接动词的动名词形式，即worth doing sth.

例 The question is not worth discussing again and again.
这个问题不值得一遍又一遍讨论。

② **It's taken me this long to understand that the cookie will never make me happy for long.**

It takes sb. (some time) to do sth. 某人花了……时间做某事

例 It takes me quite a long time to understand the meaning of the painting by Picasso.
我花了相当长的时间才理解毕加索的那幅画的意义。

for long 长久

例 We sit for long hours in front of a computer, glued to our chairs or stuck to our phones.
我们数小时地安坐在电脑面前，粘在椅子上不动窝，或者长时间拿着话筒打电话。

③ **You may not even get a chance to eat it because you are so busy just trying not to lose it.**

be busy doing sth. 忙于做某事

例 They are busy doing their homework.
他们正忙于做作业。

165

常用的还有 be busy with sth.

例 They are busy with their homework.
他们正忙于做作业。

④ Happiness does not have anything to do with the cookie; it has to do with being alive.

have something to do with　与……有关

例 Her diligence must have something with her success.
她的勤勉和她的成功一定有某些关系。

have to do with　与……有关

例 What's that have to do with it?
那跟这有什么相干？

经典名句 Famous Classics

1. Happiness is form courage.
   幸福是勇气的一种形式。

2. Happiness lies not in the mere possession of money; it lies in the joy of achievement, in the thrill of creative effort.
   幸福不在于拥有金钱，而在于获得成就时的喜悦以及产生创造力的激情。

3. Happy is the man who is living by his hobby.
   醉心于某种癖好的人是幸福的。

4. The secret of being miserable is to have leisure to bother about whether you are happy or not.
   痛苦的秘密在于有闲工夫担心自己是否幸福。

5. The supreme happiness of life is the conviction that we are loved.
   生活中最大的幸福是坚信有人爱我们。

6. There is no paradise on earth equal to the union of love and innocence.
   人间最大的幸福莫如既有爱情又清白无瑕。

7. We have no more right to consume happiness without producing

it than to consume wealth without producing it.
正像我们无权只享受财富而不创造财富一样,我们也无权只享受幸福而不创造幸福。

8. Most folks are about as happy as they make up their minds to be.
对于大多数人来说,他们认定自己有多幸福,就有多幸福。

9. Pleasure is nothing else but the intermission of pain, the enjoying of something I am in great trouble for till I have it.
快乐不过是痛苦的间歇,享受之前要进行艰苦的努力。

10. Lifetime of happiness! No man alive could bear it; it would be hell on earth.
终身幸福!这是任何活着的人都无法忍受的,那将是人间地狱。

29 Love Your Life
热爱生活

However **mean** your life is, meet it and live it; do not **shun** it and call it hard names. It is not as bad as you are. It looks poorest when you are the richest. The fault-finder will find faults in **paradise.** Love your life, poor as it is. You may perhaps have some pleasant, **thrilling**, **glorious** hours, even in a poor-house. The setting sun is reflected from the windows of the **alms-house** as brightly as from the rich man's **abode**; the snow melts before its door as early in the spring. I do not see but a quiet mind may live as **contentedly** there, and have as cheering thoughts as in a palace. The town's poor seem to me often to live the most **independent** lives of any. May be they are simply great enough to receive without **misgiving**. Most think that they are above being supported by the town; but it often happens that they are not above supporting themselves by dishonest means, which should be more **disreputable**. **Cultivate** poverty like a garden **herb**, like sage. Do not trouble yourself much to get new things, whether clothes or friends. Turn the old, return to them. Things do not change; we change. Sell your clothes and keep your **thoughts.**

不论你的生活如何卑贱，你要面对它，不要躲避它，更别用恶言咒骂它。它不像你那样坏。你最富有的时候，倒是看似最穷。爱找缺点的人就是到天堂里也能找到缺点。你要爱你的生活，尽管它贫穷。即使在一个济贫院里，你也还有愉快、高兴、光荣的时候。夕阳反射在济贫院的窗上，像反射在富户人家窗上一样光亮；在那门前，积雪同在早春融化。我只看到一个从容的人在那里也像在皇宫中一样，生活得心满意足而富有愉快的思想。城镇中的穷人，我看，倒往往是过着最独立不羁的生活。也许因为他们很伟大，所以受之无愧。大多数人以为自己是超然的，不靠城镇的支持；可是事实上他们往往是利用了不正当的手段，他们是不体面的。视贫穷如园中之花而像圣人一样耕植它吧！不要费事找新东西，无论是新的朋友或新的衣服。找旧的，回到那里去。万物不变，我们在变。你的衣服可以卖掉，但要保留你的思想。

Love Your Life 热爱生活 29

单词解析 Word Analysis

mean [miːn] *adj.* 刻薄的；残忍的

例 The little girls had locked themselves in upstairs because Mack had been mean to them.
小姑娘们把自己锁在楼上，因为麦克对她们很刻薄。

shun [ʃʌn] *v.* 避开；回避；避免

例 His friends shunned him.
他的朋友都避开他。

paradise ['pærədaɪs] *n.* 天堂

例 Hong Kong is travelers' paradise.
香港是旅游者的天堂。

thrilling ['θrɪlɪŋ] *adj.* 令人兴奋的；毛骨悚然的

例 Our wildlife trips offer a thrilling encounter with wildlife in its natural state.
野生动物园之旅使我们得以接触自然状态下的野生动物，让人感觉很刺激。

glorious ['glɔːriəs] *adj.* 光荣的；辉煌的；<口>愉快的

例 It is a task at once glorious and arduous.
这样的任务是非常光荣的，但同时也是非常艰巨的。

alms-house ['ɑːmzhˈaʊs] *n.* 济贫院，养老院

例 Eventually she had to give up her house and went into a nursing home.
最后，她不得不放弃自己的房子，进了养老院。

abode [ə'bəʊd] *n.* 住处；住所；逗留；<古>等待

例 The suspect is a person of no fixed abode.
嫌疑犯是个居无定所的人。

contentedly [kən'tentɪdli] *adv.* 心满意足地

例 My father sat puffing contentedly on his pipe.
父亲坐着，心满意足地抽着烟斗。

independent [ˌɪndɪ'pendənt] *adj.* 自主的；相互独立的，不相关联的

169

我的人生美文：那些随风飘逝的日子

例 Your questions should be independent of each other.
你的问题应该彼此无关。
Phil was now much more independent of his parents.
菲尔现在不那么依赖父母了。

misgiving [ˌmɪsˈɡɪvɪŋ] *n.* 疑虑，担心
例 She had some misgivings about what she was about to do.
她对自己即将要做的事情存有一些顾虑。

disreputable [dɪsˈrepjətəbl] *adj.* 声名狼藉的；见不得人的；不体面的
例 That dive attracts every disreputable people.
那家下流酒吧吸引声名狼藉的人。

cultivate [ˈkʌltɪveɪt] *v.* 栽培；耕作；培养；陶冶；结交（朋友）
例 He was granted many privileges to cultivate crops.
他被给予许多特权来培育农作物。

herb [hɜːb] *n.* 药草；香草
例 I had to take the herb tea although it's bitter.
虽然汤药很苦，我还是不得不喝了。

thoughts [ˈθɔːts] *n.* 思想（thought的名词复数），想法；关心；思索
例 Usually at this time our thoughts are on Christmas.
通常在这种时候，我们的心思全放在了圣诞节上。
He had given some thought to what she had told him.
他认真考虑了她对他说过的话。

语法知识点 Grammar points

① **It is not as bad as you are.**

as+adj. +as. 表示"和……一样……"

例 He is as tall as me.
他和我一样高。

② **Love your life, poor as it is.**

这是as引导的让步状语从句，表语提前。

> Hardworking as he was, he failed the exam.
> 尽管他非常用功，他还是没通过考试。

③ **May be they are simply great enough to receive without misgiving.**

enough to 足以

> McGregor's effort was enough to edge Johnson out of the top spot.
> 麦格雷戈奋力一搏，成功地将约翰逊从第一的位置上挤了下来。

④ **Most think that they are above being supported by the town; but it often happens that they are not above supporting themselves by dishonest means, which should be more disreputable.**

这是一个复合句。包含了两个that引导的宾语从句，和which引导的非限制性定语从句。其中，that引导的从句分别做think和happens的宾语。而which是关系代词，指代的是前面they are not above supporting themselves by dishonest means这一句话，在从句中充当主语。注意，非限制性定语从句应当有逗号隔开。

> I bet that you will win the game.
> 我打赌你会赢。
>
> The students don't have homework today, which makes them happy.
> 学生们今天没有作业要做，这让他们非常高兴。

经典名句 Famous Classics

1. The key is to keep company only with people who uplift you, whose presence calls forth your best.
   关键在于，只与那些能激励你的人相处，只与那些能让你全力以赴的人在一起。

2. Can miles truly separate you from friends? If you want to be with someone you love, aren't you already there?
   朋友真的会被距离分隔吗？当你想要与所爱的人在一起时，你不是已经在那里了吗？

3. Money couldn't buy friends but you got a better class of enemy.

钱不能买来朋友，但能让你的敌人更高级一些。

4. A friend is one who knows you and loves you just the same.
朋友是那些了解你，却仍然一样爱你的人。

5. Lots of people want to ride with you in the limo, but what you want is someone who will take the bus with you when the limo breaks down.
很多人都会乐意跟你一起坐在豪华轿车里，但你需要的是那些当轿车坏掉之后，愿意陪你坐公交车的人。

6. A friendship founded on business is better than a business founded on friendship.
建立在生意上的友谊，好过建立在友谊上的生意。

7. I want you to be concerned about your next door neighbor. Do you know your next door neighbor?
我希望你能够关心隔壁的邻居。你认识你隔壁的邻居吗？

8. It is wise to apply the oil of refined politeness to the mechanism of friendship.
要常给友谊这台机器用礼仪这种润滑油进行保养。

9. Happy is the man who finds a true friend, and far happier is he who finds that true friend in his wife.
幸福是你能够找到真正的朋友，而更幸福的人是发现自己的妻子就是这个朋友。

10. And when life's sweet fable ends, Soul and body part like friends, No quarrels, murmurs, no delay. A kiss, a sigh, and so away.
当甜美的人生故事结束的时候，灵魂与身体像朋友一样地告别。没有争吵、喁喁和拖延，只是一个亲吻，一声叹气，然后分隔两地。

11. In prosperity, our friends know us; in adversity, we know our friends.
在生活富足的时候，朋友们会认清我们；在生活贫困的时候，我们会认清朋友们。

12. True terror is to wake up one morning and discover that your high school class is running the country.
真正的恐惧是，你一早醒来，发现你的高中同学在统治这个国家。

30 Choosing an Occupation
选择职业

Dear Sir,

I am very sorry that the pressure of other **occupations** has prevented me from sending an earlier reply to your letter.

In my opinion a man's first duty is to find a way of supporting himself, **thereby relieving** other people of the **necessity** of supporting him. **Moreover**, the learning to do work of practical value in the world, in an exact and careful manner, is of itself, a very important education, the effects of which make themselves felt in all other **pursuits**. The habit of doing that which you do not **care** about when you would much rather be doing something else, is **invaluable**. It would have saved me a **frightful** waste of time if I had ever had it **drilled** into me in youth.

Success in any scientific career requires an **unusual** equipment of capacity, industry and energy. If you possess that equipment, you will find **leisure** enough after your daily **commercial** work is over, to make an opening in the scientific ranks for yourself. If you do not, you had better stick to **commerce**. Nothing is less to

尊敬的先生：

我非常抱歉，其他工作的压力使我没能早点回复您的信件。

在我看来，一个人的首要责任是想办法养活自己，这样就能使他人免于承担必须供养该人的负担。另外，以准确和谨慎的态度做些世上具有实用价值的工作，本身来说就是一个很重要的教育，在所有其他的追求中他们也会有所感受。即使是在你不情愿而宁肯去干点别的什么的时候，也坚持去做你不想做的事情，这种做事习惯具有无比重要的意义。如果我在年轻的时候就认识到这一点的话，那么许多的光阴就不会虚度了。

任何科学事业上的成功都要求具有非同一般的能力、勤勉和活力。如果你拥有那种能力，你会在日常商业工作结束后得到足够的乐趣，在科学等级上为自己开拓新领域。如果你没有，你最好从商。没有任何事情比一个年轻男人的命运更让人羡慕了，就像苏格兰谚语说的，"宁为玉碎，不为瓦

173

be desired than the fate of a young man who is, as the Scotch proverb says, in "trying to make a spoon or spoil a horn", and becomes a **mere** hanger-on in literature or in science, when he might have been a useful and a valuable member of Society in other occupations.

I think that your father ought to see this letter.

Yours faithfully,
T. H. Huxley

全"。当他可能在其他职业上成为对社会有用的、珍贵的人才时,他却仅仅成为了在文学或科学方面依附别人的人。

我觉得你爸爸应该看看这封信。

你的忠实的
T. H. 赫胥黎

单词解析 Word Analysis

occupation [ˌɑːkjuˈpeɪʃn] *n.* 职业;占有;消遣;居住

例 I haven't had your name and occupation yet.
我还没有你的名字和职业。

thereby [ˌðerˈbaɪ] *adv.* 因此;从而

例 I have never been to that city; thereby I don't know much about it.
我从未去过那座城市,因此对它不怎么熟悉。

relieve [rɪˈliːv] *v.* 救济;减轻;解除

例 The Government acted quickly to relieve the widespread distress caused by the earthquake.
地震造成大范围的灾难,政府迅速采取行动赈济灾民。

necessity [nəˈsesəti] *n.* 需要;必需品;必然

例 Necessity is the mother of invention.
需要是发明之母。

moreover [mɔːrˈəʊvə(r)] *adv.* 再者;此外;而且

例 A talented artist, he was, moreover, a writer of some note.
他是一位有才华的艺术家,同时也是颇有名气的作家。

Choosing an Occupation
选择职业

The task is difficult, and moreover, time is pressing.
任务艰巨，并且时间紧迫。

pursuit [pərˈsuːt] *v.* 追求；追赶；工作

例 His life is spent in the pursuit of pleasure.
他一生都在寻欢作乐。

care [ker] *v.* 关心，担心

例 You shouldn't let him go if you care about him.
如果你关心他，就不应该让他去。

invaluable [ɪnˈvæljuəbl] *adj.* 无价的；非常珍贵的

例 The painting is an invaluable treasure.
这幅画是无价之宝。

frightful [ˈfraɪtfl] *adj.* 可怕的；吓人的

例 These frightful experiences are branded on his memory.
这些可怕的经历深深印入他的记忆。

drill [drɪl] *n.* 练习；钻孔；（军事）训练

例 Listen to the first paragraph, then let them drill in teams.
听第一段，然后分组练习。

unusual [ʌnˈjuːʒuəl] *adj.* 不寻常的，不常见的

例 To be appreciated as a parent is quite unusual.
可怜天下父母心。

leisure [ˈliːʒər] *n.* 闲暇；休闲

例 Life today is compartmentalized into work and leisure.
现今生活分成工作和闲暇两部分。

commercial [kəˈmɜːʃl] *adj.* 商业的，贸易的

例 British Rail has indeed become more commercial over the past decade.
过去10年来，英国铁路确实变得更加商业化了。

175

commerce ['kɑːmɜːrs] *n.* 贸易；商业

例 Our country has been trying to broaden its commerce with other nations.
我国一直在努力扩大与其他国家的贸易往来。

mere [mɪr] *a.* 仅仅的；纯粹的

例 Don't scold him. He is a mere child.
别责备他，他只不过是个孩子。

语法知识点 *Grammar points*

① The habit of doing that which you do not dare about when you would much rather be doing something else, is invaluable.

这个句子中，句子主干是the habit is invaluable，中间部分都是修饰the habit。有一个that引导的定语从句，还有一个when引导的时间状语从句。

would much rather 宁愿

例 Fiona would much rather be among the bright lights than in the country. She loves London.
比起农村来，费奥娜更喜欢富有刺激的城市生活，她喜欢伦敦。

② It would have saved me a frightful waste of time if I had ever had it drilled into me in youth.

这个句子是虚拟语气，是同过去相反。从句用过去完成时，主句用would have done过去将来完成时（可用于虚拟句，表示与过去的事实相反），表示在过去某一时间对将来某一时刻以前所会发生的动作。

例 If you had planned ahead, you would have done better.
如果你早做打算的话，你会做得更好。

in youth 在青年时期；在年轻时

例 In youth passion is preponderant.
青春期最热情。

In youth we run into difficulty, in old age difficulty runs into us.
年轻时咱们闯进困境里去，上了年纪之后，困境冲着咱们而来。

Choosing an Occupation
选择职业 30

③ **Nothing is less to be desired than the fate of a young man who, as the Scotch proverb says, in "trying to make a spoon or spoil a horn" and becomes a mere hanger-on in literature or in science, when he might have been a useful and a valuable member of society in other occupations.**

less than 不到；少于

🈶 Even under the best conditions, we couldn't finish in less than three days.
即使在最好的情况下，我们也无法在少于三天的时间内完成。

This piece of furniture is really inexpensive with a price of less than forty dollars.
这件家具还不到四十美元，实在不贵。

as 在这意为"正如"。

🈶 Just as writing a fiction, programming is a process of creating art.
如同写小说一样，程序设计也是一个艺术创造的过程。

后面有一个when引导的时间状语从句；might have done 表示"很有可能做某事，但却没做"。

🈶 You might have done the work better.
你本来可以把工作做得更好。

He might have done it better if he had put his mind to his work.
如果他专心致志的话，他可以做得更好。

经典名句 Famous Classics

1. Anger is an acid that can do more harm to the vessel in which it is stored than to anything on which it is poured.
   愤怒是一种酸性的液体，他腐蚀盛装它的容器甚于被其泼到的物品。

2. I have been complimented many times and they always embarrass me; I always feel that they have not said enough.
   我被称赞过无数次，每次都感到十分羞愧；我总觉得他们说得还不够多。

3. Let us be moral. Let us contemplate existence.
让我们遵从道德。让我们思考自己的存在吧。

4. Any man may be in good spirits and good temper when he's well dressed. There are not much credit in that.
任何一个穿着整洁的人都能精神振奋并且和蔼可亲，他们做到这点没什么了不起。

5. The superior man is satisfied and composed; the mean man is always full of distress.
君子坦荡荡，小人长戚戚。

6. We would frequently be ashamed of our good deeds if people saw all of the motives that produced them.
如果善行背后的动机能够被别人看穿，我们会经常感到羞愧。

7. Want is one only of five giants on the road of reconstruction, the others are Disease, Ignorance, Squalor and Idleness.
欲望是阻碍国家重建的五大障碍之一，另外的有疾病、无知、腐败与懒惰。

8. The ends cannot justify the means for the simple and obvious reason that the means employed determine the nature of the ends produced.
虽然方法与手段决定了之后的结果，但不能因为结果是好的就说使用的手段也是好的。

读书笔记

31 The Rose Within
带刺的玫瑰

A certain man planted a rose and watered it **faithfully** and before it **blossomed**, he **examined** it. He saw the bud that would soon blossom, but noticed **thorns** upon the **stem** and he thought, "How can any beautiful flower come from a plant **burdened** with so many sharp thorns?" Saddened by this thought, he **neglected t**o water the rose, and just before it was ready to **bloom**, it died.

So it is with many people. Within every soul there is a rose. The God-like qualities planted in us at birth, grow **amid** the thorns of our faults. Many of us look at ourselves and see only the thorns, the **defects**. We **despair**, thinking that nothing good can possibly come from us. We neglect to water the good within us, and eventually it dies. We never realize our potential. Some people do not see the rose within themselves; someone else must show it to them. One of the greatest gifts a person can possess is to be able to reach past the thorns of another, and find the rose within them. This is the **characteristic** of love. To look at a person and, knowing his faults, recognize the **nobility** in his soul and

有一个人种了一株玫瑰，诚心诚意地浇水，在它开花之前一直仔细观察。他看到花蕾很快就要开花，但也注意到了花茎上的刺，他想："为什么美丽的花都来自负担了这么多尖锐的刺的植物呢？"因为这个想法，他感到非常悲伤，就在花要开之前，他疏忽了，没有浇水，植物就死了。

很多人都是这样。在每个人的灵魂里都有这么一株玫瑰。在我们出生时，优秀的品质把它种下，在我们犯下的错误铸成的刺中成长。我们中许多人审视自己的时候只看到那些刺，那些缺陷。我们感到绝望，觉得我们身上没有什么好的东西。我们忽视了浇灌我们本身好的那些东西，最后它们都死了。我们从未了解自身的潜能。一些人没有看到他们内心的玫瑰花；其他人就必须向他们展示。一个人能拥有的最棒的天赋之一就是可以原谅别人身上的刺，找到他们内心的玫瑰。看到一个人，了解他的缺点，欣赏他灵魂里的高贵，

我的人生美文：那些随风飘逝的日子

help him realize that he can overcome his faults. If we show him the "rose" within himself, he will **conquer** the thorns. Only then will he blossom many times over.

帮他认识到他可以克服缺点，这都是爱的体现，如果我们向他展示他心中的玫瑰，他会征服那些刺，只有那样，他才能花开不败。

单词解析 Word Analysis

faithfully ['feɪθfəli] *adv.* 忠实；诚心诚意；深信着
例 His translation follows the origin faithfully.
他的翻译忠实于原文。

blossom ['blɑːsəm] *v.* 开花；成长
例 The apple trees will blossom soon.
苹果树很快就要开花。

examine [ɪɡ'zæmɪn] *v.* 检查；调查；考试；仔细观察
例 He was unable to examine the issue with detachment.
他不能客观公正地调查这一问题。

thorn [θɔːrn] *n.* 刺；荆棘
例 She got her finger pricked by a thorn.
她的手指被刺扎了一下。

stem [stem] *n.* 柄；茎；干；船首
例 This is a plant stem that has been pithead.
这是一根已经除去木髓的植物的茎。

burden ['bɜːrdn] *v.* 使负重；装载；烦扰
例 I don't want to burden you with my problem.
我不想让我的问题给你添麻烦。

neglect [nɪ'ɡlekt] *v.* 忽略；忽视；疏忽
例 No country can afford to neglect education.
任何国家都不容忽视教育。

The Rose Within
带刺的玫瑰 31

bloom [bluːm] *v.* 开花；繁盛
- 例 The roses are blooming!
  玫瑰花正在盛开！

amid [əˈmɪd] *prep.* 在其间；在其中
- 例 He sat down amid deafening applause.
  他在震耳欲聋的掌声中就座。

defect [ˈdiːfekt] *n.* 缺点；缺陷
- 例 If it were not for this defect, I shall hire him at once.
  如果不是因为这个缺点，我会马上雇他。

despair [dɪˈspeə(r)] *v.* 绝望
- 例 I looked at my wife in despair.
  我绝望地看着妻子。

characteristic [ˌkærəktəˈrɪstɪk] *n.* 特点；特性；特色
- 例 Ambition is a characteristic of all successful businessmen.
  雄心勃勃是所有成功生意人的共同特点。

nobility [noʊˈbɪləti] *n.* 贵族；高尚
- 例 He is remembered for the nobility of his character.
  他因品质高尚而被人怀念。

conquer [ˈkɒŋkə(r)] *v.* 征服；攻克，打败（敌人）；克服
- 例 I was certain that love was quite enough to conquer our differences.
  我相信爱足以克服我们的种种差异。

语法知识点 Grammar points

① He saw the bud that would soon blossom, but noticed thorns upon the stem and he thought, "How can any beautiful flower come from a plant burdened with so many sharp thorns?"

这个句子中有一个定语从句，先行词是the bud，that在从句中充当主语。

come from 来自；起源于

例 Nothing but disaster would come from such a plan.
此计划除了失败以外将一无所获。

We heard clink come from that room.
我们听到那个屋子传来叮当声。

burdened with 担负……；抱着……

例 They were burdened with heavy taxation.
他们负担重税。

He was burdened with a large bundle of magazines.
他吃力地抱着一大捆杂志。

② **Saddened by this thought, he neglected to water the rose, and just before it was ready to bloom, it died.**

这个句子中，saddened by this thought是过去分词做伴随状语，过去分词可以做伴随状语，表示它与谓语动作同时存在或发生，saddened和he是动宾关系。

例 Compared with a quite ordinary star, like the sun, the earth is small indeed.
与一个很普通恒星如太阳相比较，地球的确很小。

The film star walked to his car, followed by a crowd of journalists.
这名影星朝他的小汽车走去，后面跟着一群新闻记者。

Judith lay on the settee, absorbed in her book.
朱迪恩躺在沙发椅上专心致志地看书。

③ **Some people do not see the rose within themselves; someone else must show it to them.**

someone else 其他人、别人

例 Criticism is useful information about how someone else perceives you.
批评是给出别人如何看待你的有用的信息。

show sth. to sb. 出示某物给某人

例 I'll show my recent photos to you.
我将给你看看我最近的照片。

The Rose Within 带刺的玫瑰 31

④ **Only then will he blossom many times over.**

这个句子是一个部分倒装的句子，only放在句首，后面的句子语序用部分倒装。

例 Only in this way can we wipe out the enemy troops.
只有这样我们才能消灭敌军。

many times over 再三

例 Revolutionary in its time, New York's GW has been surpassed many times over.
在它的时代中具有革新性，纽约华盛顿大桥的技术经久不衰。

The Huanghe River has changed its course many times over the centuries.
历史上，黄河曾经多次改道。

经典名句 Famous Classics

1. Women who seek to be equal with men lack ambition.
   想要与男人们平等是女人们缺乏雄心状态的表现。

2. There are two things that will be believed of any man whatsoever, and one of them is that he has taken to drink.
   有两件事情无论如何总会让男人们相信，其中一条就是：他们已经爱上喝酒了。

3. The fundamental defect of fathers, in our competitive society, is that they want their children to be a credit to them.
   在我们这个竞争激烈的社会上，父亲们根本的缺点是他们总想要自己的孩子给自己脸上增光。

4. Philosophers and politicians have agreed that the bonding together in family groups is both instinctive and necessary to human welfare—and therefore essential to the health of a society. The family is the microcosm.
   哲学家和政客们都一致同意，家庭对于人类既是天性，也是必需——也因而对整个社会的健康运行影响重大。家庭是一个社会的缩影。

5. One would be in less danger, From the wiles of a stranger. If one's own kin and kith, Were more fun to be with.
   如果一个人的亲朋好友是他喜爱的伴侣，那么这个人就更容易远离陌生人的诡计。

6. The hand that rocks the cradle is the hand that rules the world.
   推动摇篮的手就是支配着世界的手。

7. Children begin by loving their parents; after a time they judge them; rarely, if ever, do they forgive them.
   孩子们在一开始爱他们的父母，之后就开始指责他们，但极少数人会原谅他们。

8. It is a melancholy truth that even great men have their poor relations.
   伟人们，很不幸地，也有他们的穷亲戚。

9. A child is not a vase to be filled, but a fire to be lit.
   孩子们不是等待被填满的花瓶，而是等待被点燃的火焰。

10. Generations pass while some trees stand, and old families last not three oaks.
    几代人都去世了，但一些大树还活着，古老的显赫家族寿命也不会长过三颗橡树。

11. My father was frightened to his mother; I was frightened of my father, and I am damned well going to see to it that my children are frightened of me.
    我的父亲很害怕他的母亲，我很害怕我的父亲，我一定会让我的孩子也害怕我。

12. The affection you get back from children is sixpence give as change for a sovereign.
    孩子回报给父母的感情，就像用6个便士换来一个国家一样。

13. A slavish bondage to parents cramps every faculty of the mind.
    对父母的过于依赖会毁掉一切才能。

32 My Pain
我的痛苦

I have told you, reader, that I had learnt to love Mr. Rochester. I could not unlove him now, because I found that he had ceased to notice me—because I might pass hours in his **presence**, and he would never once turn his eyes in my direction—because I saw all his attentions appropriated by a great lady who scorned to touch me with the hem of her robes as she passed; who, if ever her dark and **imperious** eye fell on me by chance, would withdraw it instantly as from an object too mean to merit **observation**. I could not unlove him because I felt sure he would soon marry this very lady—because I read daily in her a proud security in his **intentions** respecting her—because I witnessed hourly in him a style of courtship which, if careless and choosing rather to be sought than to seek, was yet, in its very carelessness, captivating, and in its very pride, **irresistible**.

There was nothing to cool or **banish** love in these circumstances, though much to create despair. Much too, you will think, reader, to **engender jealousy**: if a woman, in my position,

我已经告诉过你，读者朋友，我意识到自己爱上了罗切斯特先生，我现在不能不爱他，仅仅因为我发现他不再关注我了——因为我可能在他面前待上几个小时，而他的眼睛从不朝我的方向瞟上一眼——因为我发现他所有的注意力被一位贵妇人所吸引，她从我身边走过时，连长袍的边都不屑于碰我一下，当她阴险专横的眼神碰巧落在我身上，她会立即避开，就像这件东西太廉价不值得她看上一眼。我不能不爱他，仅仅因为我确信不久他就会娶这位女士——因为每天我都能从她身上看出她高傲地认为她在他心目中的地位已经非常稳固——因为我每时每刻都目睹着他对她的追求，尽管漫不经心，又表现出宁愿被人追求而不追求别人，却由于随意而显得富有魅力，由于傲慢而愈发不可抗拒。

在此般情形下，任何事物都无法冷却或者浇灭我的爱，尽管这很可能会带来绝望。读者朋友，你会认为，如果一个

could presume to be jealous of a woman in Miss Ingram's. But I was not jealous or very rarely; —the nature of the pain I suffered could not be explained by that word. Miss Ingram was a mark beneath jealousy: She was too inferior to excite the feeling. Pardon the seeming **paradox**; I mean what I say.

　　She was very showy, but she was not genuine; she had a fine person, many brilliantattainments; but her mind was poor, her heart barren by nature: nothing bloomed **spontaneously** on that soil; no unforced natural fruit delighted by its freshness. She was not good; she was not original: she used to repeat sounding phrases from books: she never offered, nor had, an opinion of her own. She advocated a high tone of sentiment; but she did not know the sensations of **sympathy** and pity; tenderness and truth were not in her. Too often she betrayed this, by the undue vent she gave to a spiteful **antipathy** she had conceived against little Adele: Pushing her away with some contumelious epithet if she happened to approach her; sometimes ordering her from the room, and always treating her with coldness and **acrimony**. Other eyes besides mine watched these **manifestations** of character- watched them closely, keenly, shrewdly. Yes; the future bridegroom, Mr. Rochester

My Pain 我的痛苦 32

himself, exercised over his intended a ceaseless surveillance; and it was from this sagacity—this guardedness of his—this perfect, clear consciousness of his fair one's defects—this obvious absence of passion in his sentiments towards her, that my ever—torturing pain arose.

罗切斯特先生自己也不停地监视着他的意中人。正是这种睿智——他的这份提防——这种对自己美人缺陷的清醒全面的认识——正是他的感情对她明显缺乏热情这一点，引起了我无休止的痛苦。

单词解析 Word Analysis

presence ['prezns] *n.* 出席，到场；风度，风采
- 例 Her Majesty later honoured the Headmaster with her presence at lunch.
  随后女王陛下出席了午餐，令校长感到荣幸。

imperious [ɪm'pɪəriəs] *adj.* 专横的，飞扬跋扈的
- 例 From across the desk she gave him a witheringly imperious look.
  她从桌子对面扫了他一眼，目光咄咄逼人，凌厉而专横。

observation [ˌɒbzə'veɪʃn] *n.* 观察，观测
- 例 In hospital she'll be under observation all the time.
  医院会对她24小时密切观察。

intentions [ɪn'tenʃənz] *n.* 意图，目的，打算
- 例 Beveridge announced his intention of standing for parliament.
  贝弗里奇宣布他打算竞选议员。

irresistible [ˌɪrɪ'zɪstəbl] *adj.* 无法抗拒的，诱惑人的
- 例 It proved an irresistible temptation to Hall to go back.
  事实证明回去对霍尔是个不可抗拒的诱惑。

banish ['bænɪʃ] *v.* 放逐，驱逐；消除，排除
- 例 I was banished to the small bedroom upstairs.
  我被赶到了楼上的小卧室。

engender [in'dʒendə] v. 产生，引起
例 A talented artist, he was, moreover, a writer of some note.
他是一位有才华的艺术家，同时也是颇有名气的作家。
The task is difficult, and moreover, time is pressing.
任务艰巨，并且时间紧迫。

jealousy ['dʒeləsi] n. 妒忌
例 His life is spent in the pursuit of pleasure.
他一生都在寻欢作乐。

paradox ['pærədɒks] n. 自相矛盾的
例 The story contains many levels of paradox.
这个故事存在多重悖论。

spontaneously [spɒn'teɪnɪəslɪ] adv. 自然地，自发地，不由自主地
例 I joined in the spontaneous applause.
我跟着也自然而然地鼓起掌来。

sympathy ['sɪmpəθi] n. 同情心；同情
例 We expressed our sympathy for her loss.
我们对她的损失表示同情。

antipathy [æn'tɪpəθi] n. 反感
例 She'd often spoken of her antipathy towards London.
她常提及她对伦敦的反感。

acrimony ['ækrɪməni] n. （言语、态度等的）尖刻；讥讽；毒辣；激烈
例 The council's first meeting ended in acrimony.
委员会的首次会议以激烈的争吵而告结束。

manifestation [,mænɪfe'steɪʃn] n. 表示，显示；示威
例 New York is the ultimate manifestation of American values.
纽约是美国价值观的终极体现。

My Pain 我的痛苦 32

语法知识点 *Grammar points*

① **I could not unlove him now because I found that he had ceased to notice me—because I might pass hours in his presence, and he would never once turn his eyes in my direction—because I saw all his attentions appropriated by a great lady who scorned to touch me with the hem of her robes as she passed.**

cease to 停止；不再出现某种情况

例 The people did not cease to resist even after the fall of the capital.
即使在首都失陷以后人民也没有停止抵抗。

in one's presence 在某人面前，当着某人的面

例 Either does she flatters in one's presence or speak ill of others behind its back.
她既不当面恭维人家，也不背后说人坏话。

So if one wants to get on well among Westerners, and make people feel comfortable in one's presence, it is very important to learn good Western manners.
因此，如果想同西方人相处得很好，使人们在你的面前感到舒适，你就必须学习西方的礼节。

see sb. /sth. done 表示"看见某人或某物处于某种状态"，其中sth. /sb.与后面的 done 之间存在被动关系。

例 I have never seen the word used that way before.
我从来没有看见这个词这样用过。

I saw him knocked down by a bus.
我看见他被一辆公共汽车撞到了。

② **Who, if ever her dark and imperious eye fell on me by chance, would withdraw it instantly as from an object too mean to merit observation.**

by chance 偶然；意外地

例 I met him by chance at Canterbury Cathedral.
我是在坎特伯雷大教堂偶然地碰到过他。

③ **She used to repeat sounding phrases from books: she never offered, not had, an opinion of her own.**

of one's own 属于某人自己的

例 She had concentrated on her job of teaching other people's children. Sometimes she longed for one of her own.
她一直潜心于她的工作——教育别人的孩子，有时候她也渴望自己有个孩子。

used to 过去常常

例 They used to buy ten kilos of beef in one lump.
他们过去常买10公斤重的整块牛肉。

经典名句 Famous Classics

1. The foolish man seeks happiness in the distance; the wise grows it under his feet.
   愚者求福于远方，智者培植于脚下。

2. We define love as a delight in the presence of the other person and an affirming of his value and development as much as one's own.
   我们把爱情定义为一种和另外一个人相处时的愉悦，一种像肯定自己一样对他的价值和发展的肯定。

3. Contemporary urban life is often characterized by frequent changes in one's living space and environment, and the constant presence—whether good or bad—of excessive visual and sound stimuli.
   我们的生活空间和周围环境当中充满了变化，视觉和听觉上的刺激一刻不曾停歇（不管是好的还是坏的），正是这些造就了当代的都市生活。

4. Nothing is impossible for a willing heart.
   心之所愿，无所不成。

33 Draw a Leaf for Life
为生命画一片叶

In the **sickroom,** a young girl had **lain** in bed for almost two months. Beside her was her mother who looked pale.

"Mum, I want to take a look at the **scenery** outside the window!" said the young girl in a low voice.

With the help of her mother, she came up to the window and looked out of it, **sighing** for her lost **youth**. The wind was blowing hard, she noticed some leaves falling off a big tree outside the window.

"I am dying! As soon as all the leaves fall down, I will leave the world..." said the young girl. Watching the falling leaves, the young girl couldn't help **bursting** into tears.

From then on, the young girl's illness got worse and worse and she lost more and more color. In November, the girl's illness took a turn for the worse and she **refuse** the **treatment.**

The girl's mother was so worried that she asked her friend, who was an artist, for help. The artist had **pity** on the young girl who was dying and he felt that he must do something to help the girl. In order to save the young girl's

病房里一个小女孩躺在床上几乎2个月了，在她旁边是她的妈妈，看起来很是苍白。

"妈妈，我想看看窗外的风景！"小女孩低声说道。

在妈妈的帮助下，她来到窗边，向外望去，感叹时光的流逝。大风呼呼地吹着，她注意到窗外的一棵大树上的树叶不停地落下。

"我快死了！所有的树叶都落下时，我将会离开这个世界……"小女孩说道。看着树叶落下，小女孩不禁哭了起来。

从那时起，小女孩的病情一天不如一天，她变得越来越没有血色。11月份，小女孩的病情开始新一轮的恶化，她拒绝了治疗。

小女孩的妈妈非常担心，于是找到她的艺术家朋友请求帮助。这位艺术家非常同情小女孩的遭遇，他觉得他必须做些事情来帮助这个小女孩。为了拯救小女孩的生命，这位艺术家决定画很多很多片树叶，然后秘密地挂在树干上。

第二天，小女孩非常高兴

life, the artist decided to draw many leaves and hung them on tree **branches** by **stealth**.

The young girl was pleased to see that the tree came into leaf again the next day. She began to feel pretty hopeful about her future and began to receive treatment. She made a quick recovery from her illness. Several months later, she was out of hospital.

As long as they believe that there will always be a miracle occurred, although the slim hope, but it is **eternal** life.

地看到大树重新长满了树叶。她感觉对未来充满希望并开始接受治疗。她恢复得很快，几个月后，她就出院了。

只要心存信念，总有奇迹发生，希望虽然渺茫，但它永存人世。

单词解析 *Word Analysis*

sickroom ['sɪkru:m] *n.* 病房

例 Close friends were allowed into the sickroom.
密友可以进入病房。

lain [leɪn] （动词lie的过去分词）躺；位于；说谎

例 My father's working bench was covered with a cloth and his coffin was laid there.
爸爸的工作台上盖了一块布，他的灵柩就陈放在那儿。

scenery ['si:nəri] *n.* 风景；景色；[戏]舞台布景

例 Sometimes they just drive slowly down the lane enjoying the scenery.
有时他们只是沿着小路慢慢地开车，欣赏两旁的风景。

sigh [saɪ] *v.* 叹息，叹气

例 Roberta sighed with relief.
罗伯塔松了口气。

Draw a Leaf for Life
为生命画一片叶

youth [ju:θ] *n.* 青春；青年；青少年时期；年轻

例 In my youth my ambition had been to be an inventor.
我年轻时的抱负是成为一个发明家。

The team is now a good mixture of experience and youth.
这个队如今既经验丰富又充满朝气。

burst [bɜ:st] *v.* 爆炸；爆发，突发

例 The driver lost control when a tyre burst.
一个车胎爆了，司机失去了控制。

refuse [rɪ'fju:z] *v.* 拒绝，回绝

例 He expects me to stay on here and I can hardly refuse.
他希望我继续留在这里，我很难拒绝。

treatment ['tri:tmənt] *n.* 治疗，疗法；处理；待遇，对待

例 Many patients are not getting the medical treatment they need.
很多病人没有得到他们需要的医治。

We don't want any special treatment.
我们不想要任何特殊待遇。

pity ['pɪti] *n.* 同情，怜悯

例 I don't know whether to hate or pity him.
我不知道该恨他，还是该同情他。

branch [brɑ:ntʃ] *n.* 树枝，分支；分部；支流

例 A thrush alighted on a branch of the pine tree.
一只画眉落在松树的树枝上。

stealth [stelθ] *n.* 秘密行动；鬼祟；秘密

例 Both sides advanced by stealth.
双方都暗中向前推进。

eternal [ɪ'tɜ:nl] *adj.* 永久的；永恒的；永远的

例 Rome has been called the Eternal City.
罗马一向被称为"不朽之城"。

语法知识点 *Grammar points*

① **With the help of her mother, she came up to the window and looked out of it, sighing for her lost youth.**

sigh for sth 惋惜，思念，渴望

例 Emilia sighed for her lost youth.
伊米莉亚惋惜逝去的青春。

② **Watching the falling leaves, the young girl couldn't help bursting into tears.**

can't help doing sth. 忍不住做某事

例 I can't help thinking that we've mad a big mistake.
我不禁感到我们犯了一个大错误。
We cannot help being impressed by their zeal.
我们不由得被他们的热情感动。

③ **From then on, the young girl's illness got worse and worse and she lost more and more color.**

形容词比较级+and+形容词比较级，构成固定结构，表示"越来越……"

例 The fresh water is becoming less and less.
淡水越来越少了。
More and more wild animals are in danger because there is less and less living space for them in the world.
越来越多的野生动物处于危险境地，因为世界上供他们生存的空间越来越少了。

引申：the more... , the more...句型为"the+形容词或副词比较级，the+比较级"结构，常表示"越……，就越……"，是一个复合句，其中前面的句子是状语从句，后面的句子是主句。

例 The more he gets, the more he wants.
他越来越贪（他得到的越多，就越想要）。
The higher the ground is, the thinner the air becomes.
离地面越高，空气就越稀薄。

④ **She made a quick recovery from her illness. Several months later, she was out of hospital.**

out of hospital 出院

例 He has picked up slowly since he came out of hospital.
他自出院以来，身体恢复得很慢。

经典名句 Famous Classics

1. As long as they believe that there will always be a miracle occurred, although the slim hope, but it is eternal life.
只要心存相信，总有奇迹发生，希望虽然渺茫，但它永存人世。

2. Four short words sum up what has lifted most successful individuals above the crowd: a little bit more.
成功的秘诀就是四个简单的字：多一点点。

3. A contented mind is the greatest blessing a man can enjoy in this world.
知足是人生在世最大的幸事。

4. Health is certainly more valuable than money, because it is by health that money is procured.
健康当然比金钱更为重要，因为我们所赖以获得金钱的就是健康。

5. Miracles sometimes occur, but one has to work terribly for them.
奇迹有时候是会发生的，但是你得为之拼命地努力。

6. While there is life, there is hope.
有生命就有希望。（留得青山在，不怕没柴烧。）

7. Storms make trees take deeper roots.
风暴使树木深深扎根。

8. What makes life dreary is the want of motive.
没有了目的，生活便黯淡无光。

9. Our destiny offers not the cup of despair, but the chalice of opportunity. So let us seize it, not in fear, but in gladness.
命运给予我们的不是失望之酒，而是机会之杯。因此，让我们毫不畏惧、满心愉悦地把握命运。

10. A strong man will struggle with the storms of fate.
强者能同命运的风暴抗争。

11. The most terrible enemy is no strong belief.
最可怕的敌人，就是没有坚强的信念。

12. We must accept finite disappointment, but we must never lose infinite hope.
我们必须接受失望，因为它是有限的，但千万不可失去希望，因为它是无穷的。